BLUEPRINTS
Music
Key Stage 1
Teacher's Resource
Book

Aelwyn Pugh

Stanley Thornes (Publishers) Ltd

First published in 1994 by:
Stanley Thornes (Publishers) Ltd
Ellenborough House
Wellington Street
CHELTENHAM GL50 1YD
England

A catalogue record for this book is available from the British Library.
ISBN 0–7487–1640–8

Typeset by Tech-Set, Gateshead, Tyne & Wear
Printed and bound in Great Britain at The Bath Press, Avon

CONTENTS

INTRODUCTION

WHAT IS *BLUEPRINTS: MUSIC?*

Blueprints: Music is a practical resource for teachers which has been written to help fulfil the requirements of the National Curriculum. It may be used flexibly, either as an ideas bank or as a core resource for the whole subject. The book has been designed so that all class teachers may use it, whatever their experience in music. It may be used both by those teachers who feel inexperienced and lack confidence in music and by specialists. It can also be helpful in the production of a whole school music policy. *Blueprints: Music* could be used equally well by teachers and schools not following the National Curriculum.

Blueprints: Music consists of materials for Key Stages 1 and 2. There is a Teacher's Resource Book, a book of Pupils' Copymasters and an accompanying cassette of songs for each Key Stage.

Blueprints: Music Key Stage 1 and the National Curriculum

Blueprints: Music Key Stage 1 aims to provide a core resource for National Curriculum Music that can be used by non-specialist teachers as well as by specialists. (You will find the requirements for National Curriculum Music set out on pages vii–ix.) The Attainment Targets in music are more general than those for other National Curriculum foundation subjects. This has the advantage of simplicity. A lack of detail, however, does not always make life easier, especially for those teachers who may now be having to teach music for the first time in their careers. The Non-Statutory Guidance, although claiming to be 'written with the non-specialist in mind', in practice, needs considerable explanation in order to be useful to its audience. *Blueprints: Music Key Stage 1* aims to give the necessary extra guidance. The aim has been to provide a sequence of activities which will cover all the requirements of the ATs and PoS.

Blueprints: Music Key Stage 1

Blueprints: Music Key Stage 1 consists of the Teacher's Resource Book, a Pupils' Copymaster book and an accompanying cassette of songs. It is not essential to have all three components because you can use the Teacher's Resource Book on its own. They have been designed, however, to be used together as a satisfying and complete package.

This Teacher's Resource Book is the main resource, comprising a brief guide to National Curriculum Music,

notes on performing, listening and composing, a bank of music activities, and a glossary of musical terms.

Music activities for Key Stage 1 form the core of the book. They form a bank of structured and progressive ideas for music work, starting with very first activities for use with reception children and progressing to more advanced work for older infants. Each activity helps to develop concepts or skills and provides a complete lesson with clearly defined objectives and instructions on how to carry it out. Many activities also include ideas for extension work which can be adapted to suit the varying needs and abilities of the pupils. Listening activities are included throughout.

Many of the activities are supported by pupils' copymasters. These photocopiable sheets function as visual prompts to musical activity. Many of the copymasters can be used as 'flashcards' to stimulate class discussion. These cards are intended to accustom children to interpreting visual clues in preparation for later work on reading music notation. A few copymasters serve as pupils' worksheets and still others are to be used as pictorial musical scores.

You will find that all the songs to be taught are included on the accompanying cassette. The music for these songs is included in the Teacher's Resource Book. Do not be discouraged by the presence of the music! You can make sense of everything in this book without referring to it, as long as you have the cassette. You will find that the cassette is referred to throughout by this symbol: [cassette icon] The musical arrangements have been recorded so that the voice is in only one speaker and can be turned off if necessary. Copymasters are referred to by this symbol: [C1–5 icon] You will also find a few sample copymasters included at the back of the book for your interest.

You will also find a short section on performing, listening and composing. These are the three main focal points of music teaching as identified by the National Curriculum. This section gives you general, practical advice on all aspects of these three areas: performing (singing, choosing and using instruments at Key Stage 1), developing listening skills, and composing. Detailed practical activities for each of these areas are included in the music activities section.

How to use this book

You will want to look at the 'Performing, listening and composing' section for general advice on activities, resources and possible teaching strategies. The main music activities section, however, will provide you with the practical activities that you will use in the classroom.

These activities are arranged in a progressive and developmental way. Starting with simple finger rhymes, they build up to the point where children are able to compose their own music; perform an increasing range of songs; and understand, talk about and identify a range of concepts as they sing, play and listen to their own and others' music. They will also gradually acquire pre-notational skills which will eventually enable them to read and write music.

Any child who progresses through the book from beginning to end, during its infant school days, will have had the opportunity to participate in the full range of activities suggested in the KS1 Programme of Study, and of addressing both National Curriculum Attainment Targets for Music. The precise relationship between each activity and National Curriculum requirements and guidance is set out in the charts on pages xi–xxiii.

There is enough material included in this book to allow children to pursue at least one lesson per week of music throughout their infant years. Reception teachers are advised to focus on activities 1–40; Y1 teachers on activities 40–80 and Y2 teachers on the remaining materials. These divisions are approximate and activities on each side of the break point may still be useful. Precisely how many activities you do actually pursue during any one year will depend, as with any subject, on the abilities and experiences of children in the particular class.

You will see from the charts on pages xi–xxiii that activities and concepts are constantly revisited. You can be confident that you are helping children to build on and reinforce earlier experiences, and are preparing them for skills necessary at later stages in their musical development.

The way you use this book will also depend on your own experiences, skills and confidence. The suggestions in the 'Performing, listening and composing' section will help you address some of these issues, as will the detailed advice on presentation included in each activity.

If, like many teachers, you consider yourself to be a musical novice, it might be an idea to adopt the following suggestions on how to use the book:

- Look at the section which relates most closely to the age group which you are teaching. (For example, if you are a Year 1 teacher, start by looking at the middle third of the activities and a few activities preceding that section.)
- Within that set of activities, look for a song with which you may already be familiar or the words of which you know. Or, choose one of the games which you feel that you could lead without too much difficulty.
- Prepare and present that activity.
- If that has gone fairly well (and remember, you are just starting, so do not be too harsh on yourself) try an extension of the activity if there is one included in that section. Alternatively, look at the planning chart and try another similar idea. For example, if you have been successful at the activities in Miss Muffet (No 40), you might follow it up with Jack and Jill (No. 44) because both of these involve telling the story of a well-known rhyme through music. If you look at the planning chart for those activities, you will notice that they address a range of concepts. One of these is the concept of dynamics (loud and soft). You might now decide that you want to help your children improve their grasp of that concept. In which case, by referring to the chart, you will see a whole range of activities which also address that concept. If your children have experienced some difficulty with it, try some of the activities earlier on in the book which relate to loud and soft. On the other hand, if you feel that your children need to be provided with more demanding activities relating to dynamics, try related activities at a later point in the book.

Whatever activity you choose, it is highly unlikely that it will focus on only one concept or area of experience. Therefore, you can be confident that, as you extend the depth of your pupils' experiences, you will also be extending the breadth of their experiences.

Whatever approach you take, make sure that you refer to the charts on pages xi–xxiii frequently to ensure that you are covering the full range of foci identified in National Curriculum Music.

Blueprints: Music may not be the only musical resource that you are using with your class. In which case, you could use it as an ideas bank and dip into it in order to develop or reinforce experiences encountered in the other resources available to you.

During the first year of using the book, you will be able to familiarise yourself with it and build up your confidence and skills, so that eventually you and your colleagues will be able to pursue a full range of activities from beginning to end and use it to form the basis of a whole school music policy.

GUIDE TO NATIONAL CURRICULUM MUSIC KEY STAGE 1

Music is a foundation subject within the National Curriculum at Key Stages 1 to 3. It has two Attainment Targets:

AT1: Performing and composing
AT2: Listening and appraising.

Each Attainment Target has End of Key Stage Statements which are based on a number of Strands. There are also Programmes of Study which define what pupils need to do to meet the demands of the End of Key Stage Statements.

Teachers are expected to take an integrated approach to the two ATs, to combine and interrelate them constantly. It is intended that, when the Assessment Order is published, there will be a weighting of 2 to 1 in favour of AT1: Performing and composing. It is clear, therefore, that when teachers plan and deliver their work, they should emphasise practical activities. Theory should be a means to an end, developing from and supporting the practical activities, rather than becoming an end in itself.

The Strands, End of Key Stage Statements and Programmes of Study for Key Stage 1 have been brought together in the following table:

General requirements for programmes of study

1. In all key stages, pupils should be given opportunities to:
   - undertake a balanced programme of activities which builds on previous work and takes account of previous achievement;
   - work individually, in groups, and as a whole class;
   - make appropriate use of information technology; to create and record music.

2. Pupils should perform and listen to music in a variety of genres and styles, from different periods and cultures. The repertoire chosen should be broad and designed to extend pupils' musical experiences and knowledge. It should include examples of works taken from:
   - the European 'classical' tradition, from its earliest roots to the present day;
   - folk and popular music;
   - music of the countries and regions of the British Isles;
   - a variety of cultures, Western and non-Western.

3. The repertoire selected for performance should be progressively more demanding and chosen in the light of pupils' needs, backgrounds and stages of musical development.

Attainment Target 1: Performing and composing

The development of the ability to perform and compose music with understanding.

Programme of study (relating to attainment target 1).

Strands (from the Non-Statutory Guidance)	End of Key Stage statements	Programme of study
Playing and singing (by ear, from signs and notations)	By the end of key stage 1, pupils should be able to: a) perform simple rhythmic and melodic patterns by ear and from symbols.	Pupils should: i) memorise and internalise short musical patterns and simple songs, and imitate and recall simple rhythms and melodies. ii) read simple signs and symbols and perform from them.
Controlling sounds made by the voice and a range of musical instruments	b) sing in a group and play simple instruments demonstrating some control of the sounds made.	iii) sing a variety of simple unison songs with some control of breathing, dynamics and pitch. iv) develop the technical skills needed to control the sounds of a range of tuned and untuned instruments, through playing simple pieces and accompaniments.
Performing with others		v) practise and rehearse, responding to direction. vi) share their music-making, presenting their performances effectively to different audiences, for different purposes, and in a number of places with different acoustics. vii) take part in simple vocal and instrumental improvisations, compositions and arrangements.
Composing, arranging and improvising	c) investigate, choose and combine sounds to produce simple compositions.	viii) explore and use a range of sound sources including their voices, bodies, sounds from the environment and instruments, tuned and untuned. ix) create, select and organise sounds in response to different stimuli.
Refining, recording and communicating musical ideas	d) record their own compositions and communicate them to others.	x) communicate simple musical ideas. xi) use and understand simple signs and symbols for musical sounds when composing. xii) record their own compositions.

Attainment Target 2: Listening and appraising

The development of the ability to listen to and appraise music, including knowledge of musical history, our diverse musical heritage, and a variety of other musical traditions.

Programme of study (relating to attainment target 2).

Strands (from the Non-Statutory Guidance)

End of Key Stage statements

By the end of key stage 1, pupils should be able to:

Programme of study

Pupils should:

Listening and identifying musical elements and structures

a) listen attentively and respond to short pieces of music from different times and cultures and in different styles, showing an awareness of differences and similarities.

i) learn to listen with care and concentration to their own and others' music, and make broad distinctions within the main musical elements of:

pitch	– high/low
duration	– pulse; rhythm; long/short sounds
pace	– fast/slow
timbre	– quality of sound
texture	– one sound/several sounds
dynamics	– loud/quiet
structure	– pattern; phrasing; repetition/contrast
silence	

ii) listen to, discover, make, compare and talk about everyday sounds of all kinds.

iii) respond to the musical elements, character and mood of a piece of music, by means of movement, dance, or other forms of expression.

The history of music: its composers and traditions
Appraising music: appreciation of live and recorded music

b) talk in simple but appropriate terms about sounds and music they have made, listened to, performed or composed.

iv) listen to and talk about a variety of live and recorded music exhibiting contrasts of style, including works by well-known composers and performers as well as their own and others' compositions and improvisations.

v) discuss how sounds and rhythms are used in music to achieve particular effects, and learn to recognise some different characteristics in music from different times and places.

DEVELOPING MUSICAL CONCEPTS

In developing reading and writing skills, most children progress from the concrete to the abstract. Consider, for example, how they come to read and write the word for 'cup'.

Firstly, the child will come across a cup in everyday life, will touch it, handle it, play with it. Gradually it will learn that this object has a word attached to it and will begin to call the object a 'cup'. At first, it might think that the word applies to one specific cup only, such as its favourite drinking cup. Gradually, however, it will learn that the word is actually applied to a whole range of objects which might differ considerably from each other in terms of size, shape, texture, colour and materials from which they are made.

The next stage might be for the child to see pictures of objects which it comes to recognise as cups and to which it applies the term 'cup'. At a later stage, the child might be given not only a picture of a cup but also a card with the word 'cup' written on it.

The child might now be involved in short matching games in which pictures of objects are allied to the words which represent them. The child is now at an early stage of reading. The next stage will be for the child to identify the word independently of the picture. Eventually the child will be able to write it as well as read it, applying both skills in a variety of contexts.

A similar pattern of progression from the concrete to the abstract can also be applied to the development of reading and writing skills in music and such an approach is employed in this book.

Take, for example, the pattern of progression used to enable children to learn how to represent high and low sounds. The first stage will be for children to have experience of singing a variety of songs involving both high and low sounds. From there, they will progress to singing songs which have specific reference to the word 'high' on a high pitched note and reference to the word 'low' on the low pitched note. (See, for example, 'Sometimes I reach up high'). To reinforce the concept, the children will make high or low gestures to match the appropriate words.

From there they will progress to listening to high and low sounds independently of a song. For example, as a high chime bar is sounded, they will reach up high. As a low pitched chime bar is sounded, they will crouch down low. At this stage, they are converting sounds into signs – a preliminary activity which will eventually lead to the writing of music. The same approach can also be applied to converting signs into sounds. Thus a teacher could make a high reaching gesture which the pupil then has to match by playing a high sounding chime bar. Later the activity could be extended so that three children stand in a row reaching up or crouching down. Another child could then 'read' the row of children and convert the pattern that they are creating into a sequence of high or low sounds.

By playing a variety of games based on this principle, the children will develop security in identifying high and low pitch and in reproducing them through playing or singing.

The next stage will be for the live body gestures to be replaced by pictures of people reaching high or crouching low. These can be mounted on cards and used in several ways.

First, they can be held up by the teacher so that the children can decide whether they represent high or low sounds and produce the appropriate sound accordingly (converting signs into sounds = reading). Secondly, the children could listen to a sound, decide whether it is high or low and choose the appropriate card to represent the sound (converting sounds into signs = writing). By making several copies of the copymaster, the children can be provided with the means of 'reading' and 'writing' sequences of sounds which can become increasingly longer and more complicated.

From here, it is possible to progress to adding a further sound – a 'middle' sound which is neither high nor low. Again it is possible to follow a sequence from live bodily representation to card indicators which can be used as a preliminary method of reading and writing sounds.

The present book does not take children very much further than this stage. A firm foundation will have been provided, however, which should enable your children eventually to make the transition to using more conventional symbols of staff notation.

The same method of progressing from the concrete to the abstract and of ensuring that, at each stage, children have the opportunity to convert signs into sounds and sounds into signs is also used for other musical concepts in this book. In some instances, for example in approaching loud and soft sounds, the children do actually progress to the stage of using conventional signs.

SKILL
DEVELOPMENT
GRID

Attainment Target 1: Performing and composing

The development of the ability to perform and compose music with understanding.

End of Key Stage statements / PROGRAMMES OF STUDY — ACTIVITY	a) perform simple rhythmic and melodic patterns by ear and from symbols.		b) sing in a group and play simple instruments demonstrating some control of the sounds made.					c) investigate, choose and combine sounds to produce simple compositions.			d) record their own compositions and communicate them to others.	
Pupils should:	i) memorise and internalise short musical patterns and simple songs, and imitate and recall simple rhythms and melodies.	ii) read simple signs and symbols and perform from them.	iii) sing a variety of simple unison songs with some control of breathing, dynamics and pitch.	iv) develop the technical skills needed to control the sounds of a range of tuned and untuned instruments, through playing simple pieces and accompaniments.	v) practise and rehearse, responding to direction.	vi) share their music-making, presenting their performances effectively to different audiences, for different purposes, and in a number of places with different acoustics.	vii) take part in simple vocal and instrumental improvisations, compositions and arrangements.	viii) explore and use a range of sound sources including their voices, bodies, sounds from the environment and instruments, tuned and untuned.	ix) create, select and organise sounds in response to different stimuli.	x) communicate simple musical ideas.	xi) use and understand simple signs and symbols for musical sounds when composing.	xii) record their own compositions.
1. Finger Dance	●											
2. Clap Hands	●											
3. Handy Dandy	●											
4. Matching Timbre Game												
5. Hob Shoe												
6. Music About Horses	●											
7. Fast and Slow												
8. Metronome Game												
9. Listening For Speed												
10. Cobbler, Cobbler	●											
11. Pass the Music Bag	●											
12. Pat-A-Cake	●											
13. Loud and Soft Game												
14. Listening for Volume												
15. Rock a Bye Baby	●		●	●	●			●	●			
16. Lullaby Composition							●	●	●			
17. Soft and Loud Sounds on One Instrument												
18. Loud and Soft Sounds Around Us												
19. Peter Hammers With One Hammer	●											
20. We'll Clap Hands Together	●		●									
21. What Sounds Can We Make?								●				
22. What Can We Do With Our Hands?	●		●		●			●				

Attainment Target 2: Listening and appraising

The development of the ability to listen to and appraise music, including knowledge of musical history, our diverse musical heritage, and a variety of other musical traditions.

| End of Key Stage statements | By the end of key stage 1, pupils should be able to: a) listen attentively and respond to short pieces of music from different times and cultures and in different styles, showing an awareness of differences and similarities. | | b) talk in simple but appropriate terms about sounds and music they have made, listened to, performed or composed. |

Pupils should: i) learn to listen with care and concentration to their own and others' music, and make broad distinctions within the main musical elements of:

ACTIVITY	pitch – high/low	duration – pulse; rhythm; long/short sounds	pace – fast/slow	timbre – quality of sound	texture – one sound/several sounds	dynamics – loud/quiet	structure – pattern; phrasing; repetition/contrast	silence	iii) listen to, discover, make, compare and talk about everyday sounds of all kinds.	ii) respond to the musical elements, character and mood of a piece of music, by means of movement, dance, or other forms of expression.	iv) listen to and talk about a variety of live and recorded music exhibiting contrasts of style, including works by well-known composers and performers as well as their own and others' compositions and improvisations.	v) discuss how sounds and rhythms are used in music to achieve particular effects, and learn to recognise some different characteristics in music from different times and places
1. Finger Dance		●								●		
2. Clap Hands		●								●		
3. Handy Dandy	●	●								●		
4. Matching Timbre Game				●					●			
5. Hob Shoe	✗	●								●		
6. Music About Horses	✗	●										●
7. Fast and Slow									●			
8. Metronome Game									●			
9. Listening for Speed			●									●
10. Cobbler, Cobbler	✗ ●	●	●						●	●		
11. Pass the Music Bag				●					●			
12. Pat-A-Cake	✗	●								●		
13. Loud And Soft Game									●			
14. Listening for Volume						●						●
15. Rock a Bye Baby	●					●				●	●	
16. Lullaby Composition												
17. Soft and Loud Sounds on One Instrument									●			
18. Loud and Soft Sounds Around Us						●			●			●
19. Peter Hammers With One Hammer										●		
20. We'll Clap Hands Together										●		
21. What Sounds Can We Make?												
22. What Can We Do With Our Hands?												

Attainment Target 1: Performing and composing

The development of the ability to perform and compose music with understanding.

End of Key Stage statements / ACTIVITY	a) perform simple rhythmic and melodic patterns by ear and from symbols.		b) sing in a group and play simple instruments demonstrating some control of the sounds made.				c) investigate, choose and combine sounds to produce simple compositions.				d) record their own compositions and communicate them to others.	
PROGRAMMES OF STUDY — Pupils should:	i) memorise and internalise short musical patterns and simple songs, and imitate and recall simple rhythms and melodies.	ii) read simple signs and symbols and perform from them.	iii) sing a variety of simple unison songs with some control of breathing, dynamics and pitch.	iv) develop the technical skills needed to control the sounds of a range of tuned and untuned instruments, through playing simple pieces and accompaniments.	v) practise and rehearse, responding to direction.	vi) share their music-making, presenting their performances effectively to different audiences, for different purposes, and in a number of places with different acoustics.	vii) take part in simple vocal and instrumental improvisations, compositions and arrangements.	viii) explore and use a range of sound sources including their voices, bodies, sounds from the environment and instruments, tuned and untuned.	ix) create, select and organise sounds in response to different stimuli.	x) communicate simple musical ideas.	xi) use and understand simple signs and symbols for musical sounds when composing.	xii) record their own compositions.
23. See-Saw Down on the Floor	●		●	●								
24. Composing with Body Sounds							●	●	●	●		
25. See-Saw Margery Daw	●	●	●	●								
26. Humpty Dumpty	●						●	●	●	●		
27. March March	●											
28. The Magic Instruments												
29. Goosey Goosey Gander	●	●	●									
30. Music About Birds												
31. Identifying Instruments	●											
32. Who Will Come Into Our Little Ring?	●		●									
33. Five Little Ducks	●	●	●	●								
34. Row, Row, Row the Boat	●		●	●								
35. Music Which Describes Water												
36. Wee Willy Winky	●		●			●						
37. 'Walking' or 'Runing' Music?												
38. Where Am I?								●				
39. Copy Cat Game 1								●				
40. Little Miss Muffet	●		●				●	●	●		●	●
41. Listening to Scary Music												
42. Little Bo Peep	●		●									
43. Copy Cat Game 2		●										
44. Jack and Jill	●		●			●	●	●	●	●		●

Attainment Target 2: Listening and appraising

The development of the ability to listen to and appraise music, including knowledge of musical history, our diverse musical heritage, and a variety of other musical traditions.

End of Key Stage statements	By the end of key stage 1, pupils should be able to: a) listen attentively and respond to short pieces of music from different times and cultures and in different styles, showing an awareness of differences and similarities.											b) talk in simple but appropriate terms about sounds and music they have made, listened to, performed or composed.
PROGRAMMES OF STUDY / ACTIVITY	Pupils should: i) learn to listen with care and concentration to their own and others' music, and make broad distinctions within the main musical elements of: **pitch** – high/low	**duration** – pulse; rhythm; long/short sounds	**pace** – fast/slow	**timbre** – quality of sound	**texture** – one sound/several sounds	**dynamics** – loud/quiet	**structure** – pattern; phrasing; repetition/contrast	**silence**	ii) listen to, discover, make, compare and talk about everyday sounds of all kinds.	iii) respond to the musical elements, character and mood of a piece of music, by means of movement, dance, or other forms of expression.	iv) listen to and talk about a variety of live and recorded music exhibiting contrasts of style, including works by well-known composers and performers as well as their own and others' compositions and improvisations.	v) discuss how sounds and rhythms are used in music to achieve particular effects, and learn to recognise some different characteristics in music from different times and places
23. See-Saw Down on the Floor	●									●		
24. Composing with Body Sounds												●
25. See-Saw Margery Daw	●									●		
26. Humpty Dumpty										●		
27. March March			●							●	●	
28. The Magic Instruments				●						●		
29. Goosey Goosey Gander	●									●		
30. Music About Birds	●									●		●
31. Identifying Instruments		●		●						●		
32. Who Will Come Into Our Little Ring?										●		
33. Five Little Ducks				●						●		●
34. Row, Row, Row the Boat										●		
35. Music Which Describes Water												●
36. Wee Willy Winky	●		●							●		●
37. 'Walking' or 'Runing' Music?			●									●
38. Where Am I?									●			
39. Copy Cat Game 1		●										
40. Little Miss Muffet										●		
41. Listening to Scary Music												●
42. Little Bo Peep									●			
43. Copy Cat Game 2												
44. Jack and Jill	X	●	●			●				●		

Attainment Target 1: Performing and composing

The development of the ability to perform and compose music with understanding.

End of Key Stage statements	a) perform simple rhythmic and melodic patterns by ear and from symbols.		b) sing in a group and play simple instruments demonstrating some control of the sounds made.					c) investigate, choose and combine sounds to produce simple compositions.			d) record their own compositions and communicate them to others.	
PROGRAMMES OF STUDY / ACTIVITY — Pupils should:	i) memorise and internalise short musical patterns and simple songs, and imitate and recall simple rhythms and melodies.	ii) read simple signs and symbols and perform from them.	iii) sing a variety of simple unison songs with some control of breathing, dynamics and pitch.	iv) develop the technical skills needed to control the sounds of a range of tuned and untuned instruments, through playing simple pieces and accompaniments.	v) practise and rehearse, responding to direction.	vi) share their music-making, presenting their performances effectively to different audiences, for different purposes, and in a number of places with different acoustics.	vii) take part in simple vocal and instrumental improvisations, compositions and arrangements.	viii) explore and use a range of sound sources including their voices, bodies, sounds from the environment and instruments, tuned and untuned.	ix) create, select and organise sounds in response to different stimuli.	x) communicate simple musical ideas.	xi) use and understand simple signs and symbols for musical sounds when composing.	xii) record their own compositions.
45. High and Low												
46. Listening for Pitch												
47. Teddy Bear, Teddy Bear	●	●	●			●						
48. Long and Short Sounds								●				
49. Short Short Long	●	●										
50. Listening to Long and Short Sounds												
51. Ride a Cock Horse	●		●	●		●						
52. Walking, Galloping and Trotting Patterns												
53. Horse in Music												
54. Guide to Rhythmic Notation		●										
55. Echo Activities	●											
56. Listening to Echoes												
57. Swinging Song	●		●	●		●						
58. Echo Clapping	●											
59. London Bridge is Falling Down	●		●	●		●						
60. Music About London												
61. Cumulative Echoing	●											
62. Loud and Soft Games 1	●		●		●							
63. Listening to Accented Beats												
64. Loud and Soft Games 2	●		●									
65. Listening for Contrasts in Volume												
66. Rhythm Picture Notation	●	●										

Attainment Target 2: Listening and appraising

The development of the ability to listen to and appraise music, including knowledge of musical history, our diverse musical heritage, and a variety of other musical traditions.

End of Key Stage statements	By the end of key stage 1, pupils should be able to: a) listen attentively and respond to short pieces of music from different times and cultures and in different styles, showing an awareness of differences and similarities.											b) talk in simple but appropriate terms about sounds and music they have made, listened to, performed or composed.
ACTIVITY / PROGRAMMES OF STUDY	i) learn to listen with care and concentration to their own and others' music, and make broad distinctions within the main musical elements of: **pitch** – high/low	**duration** – pulse; rhythm; long/short sounds	**pace** – fast/slow	**timbre** – quality of sound	**texture** – one sound/several sounds	**dynamics** – loud/quiet	**structure** – pattern; phrasing: repetition/contrast	**silence**	i) listen to, discover, make, compare and talk about everyday sounds of all kinds	iii) respond to the musical elements, character and mood of a piece of music, by means of movement, dance, or other forms of expression.	iv) listen to and talk about a variety of live and recorded music exhibiting contrasts of style, including works by well-known composers and performers as well as their own and others' compositions and improvisations.	v) discuss how sounds and rhythms are used in music to achieve particular effects, and learn to recognise some different characteristics in music from different times and places
45. High and Low	●									●		
46. Listening for Pitch	●											●
47. Teddy Bear, Teddy Bear	●									●		●
48. Long and Short Sounds	X	●							●			
49. Short Short Long												●
50. Listening to Long and Short Sounds												●
51. Ride a Cock Horse			●							●		
52. Walking, Galloping and Trotting Patterns									●			
53. Horse in Music												●
54. Guide to Rhythmic Notation												
55. Echo Activities						●						
56. Listening to Echoes						●						●
57. Swinging Song					●					●		
58. Echo Clapping												
59. London Bridge is Falling Down										●		
60. Music About London			●			●					●	
61. Cumulative Echoing												
62. Loud and Soft Games 1									●			
63. Listening to Accented Beats						●				●		
64. Loud and Soft Games 2												
65. Listening for Contrasts in Volume						●						●
66. Rhythm Picture Notation												

Attainment Target 1: Performing and composing

The development of the ability to perform and compose music with understanding.

End of Key Stage statements	a) perform simple rhythmic and melodic patterns by ear and from symbols.		b) sing in a group and play simple instruments demonstrating some control of the sounds made.					c) investigate, choose and combine sounds to produce simple compositions.			d) record their own compositions and communicate them to others.	
PROGRAMMES OF STUDY — Pupils should:	i) memorise and internalise short musical patterns and simple songs, and imitate and recall simple rhythms and melodies.	ii) read simple signs and symbols and perform from them.	iii) sing a variety of simple unison songs with some control of breathing, dynamics and pitch.	iv) develop the technical skills needed to control the sounds of a range of tuned and untuned instruments, through playing simple pieces and accompaniments.	v) practise and rehearse, responding to direction.	vi) share their music-making, presenting their performances effectively to different audiences, for different purposes, and in a number of places with different acoustics.	vii) take part in simple vocal and instrumental improvisations, compositions and arrangements.	viii) explore and use a range of sound sources including their voices, bodies, sounds from the environment and instruments, tuned and untuned.	ix) create, select and organise sounds in response to different stimuli.	x) communicate simple musical ideas.	xi) use and understand simple signs and symbols for musical sounds when composing.	xii) record their own compositions.
ACTIVITY												
67. More Magic Movements					●			●				
68. Zadok The Priest												
69. Follow My Leader's Accents	●			●								
70. Who is Making the Loudest Sound			●									
71. Listening to Soloists												
72. The Grand Old Duke of York	●		●									
73. More Picture Notation		●										
74. Sometimes I Reach Up High	●		●									
75. Consolidating Pitch Discrimination												
76. Who Am I? Volume Clues				●		●						
77. Who Am I? Rhythm Clues		●										
78. Human Notes		●										
79. Oranges and Lemons	●	●	●	●		●		●				
80. Music Based on Bells												
81. Picture Notation for Extended Rhymes		●										
82. Diddle Diddle Dumpling	●		●	●								
83. Chime Bars – Low to High												
84. Listening to Marches												
85. Hickory Dickory Dock	●		●	●		●		●		●		
86. Hickory Dickory Composition							●	●	●	●	●	●
87. Picture Rhythms with Silences		●										
88. Big Clocks and Little Clocks	●		●	●		●	●					

Attainment Target 2: Listening and appraising

The development of the ability to listen to and appraise music, including knowledge of musical history, our diverse musical heritage, and a variety of other musical traditions.

| End of Key Stage statements | By the end of key stage 1, pupils should be able to: a) listen attentively and respond to short pieces of music from different times and cultures and in different styles, showing an awareness of differences and similarities. | | | | | | | | | | b) talk in simple but appropriate terms about sounds and music they have made, listened to, performed or composed. | |

PROGRAMMES OF STUDY / ACTIVITY	Pupils should: i) learn to listen with care and concentration to their own and others' music, and make broad distinctions within the main musical elements of: pitch – high/low	duration – pulse; rhythm; long/short sounds	pace – fast/slow	timbre – quality of sound	texture – one sound/several sounds	dynamics – loud/quiet	structure – pattern; phrasing; repetition/contrast	silence	ii) listen to, discover, make, compare and talk about everyday sounds of all kinds.	iii) respond to the musical elements, character and mood of a piece of music, by means of movement, dance, or other forms of expression.	iv) listen to and talk about a variety of live and recorded music exhibiting contrasts of style, including works by well-known composers and performers as well as their own and others' compositions and improvisations.	v) discuss how sounds and rhythms are used in music to achieve particular effects, and learn to recognise some different characteristics in music from different times and places
67. More Magic Movements												
68. Zadok The Priest						●						
69. Follow My Leader's Accents										●		
70. Who is Making the Loudest Sound						●						
71. Listening to Soloists					●							
72. The Grand Old Duke of York	●									●		
73. More Picture Notation												
74. Sometimes I Reach Up High	●									●		
75. Consolidating Pitch Discrimination									●			
76. Who Am I? Volume Clues									●			
77. Who Am I? Rhythm Clues	✗	●										
78. Human Notes												
79. Oranges and Lemons										●		
80. Music Based on Bells												●
81. Picture Notation for Extended Rhymes												
82. Diddle Diddle Dumpling										●		
83. Chime Bars – Low to High	●											
84. Listening to Marches	●											
85. Hickory Dickory Dock										●		
86. Hickory Dickory Composition												
87. Picture Rhythms with Silences								●				
88. Big Clocks and Little Clocks					●							

Attainment Target 1: Performing and composing

The development of the ability to perform and compose music with understanding.

End of Key Stage statements / PROGRAMMES OF STUDY / ACTIVITY	a) perform simple rhythmic and melodic patterns by ear and from symbols.		b) sing in a group and play simple instruments demonstrating some control of the sounds made.					c) investigate, choose and combine sounds to produce simple compositions.		d) record their own compositions and communicate them to others.		
Pupils should:	i) memorise and internalise short musical patterns and simple songs, and imitate and recall simple rhythms and melodies.	ii) read simple signs and symbols and perform from them.	iii) sing a variety of simple unison songs with some control of breathing, dynamics and pitch.	iv) develop the technical skills needed to control the sounds of a range of tuned and untuned instruments, through playing simple pieces and accompaniments.	v) practise and rehearse, responding to direction.	vi) share their music-making, presenting their performances effectively to different audiences, for different purposes, and in a number of places with different acoustics.	vii) take part in simple vocal and instrumental improvisations, compositions and arrangements.	viii) explore and use a range of sound sources including their voices, bodies, sounds from the environment and instruments, tuned and untuned.	ix) create, select and organise sounds in response to different stimuli.	x) communicate simple musical ideas.	xi) use and understand simple signs and symbols for musical sounds when composing.	xii) record their own compositions.
89. Music About Clocks												
90. Coming Nearer and Moving Away												
91. Sounds Approaching and Departing												
92. First and Last Note Pitch Game		/										
93. Picture Rhythms with Silent Gestures		●										
94. Am I Moing Towards You or Am I Moving Away?												
95. Picture Notation Without Words		●										
96. Hunt the Thimble			●			●						
97. Smooth Snakes			●	●								
98. Let's Make a Crescendo							●					
99. Volume Listening Activity												
100. Leaping Frogs	●	●	●									
101. 'Smooth' and 'Leaping' Melodies												
102. Let's Make a Diminuendo					●		●					●
103. Steps and Leaps			●									
104. Spot the Tune From It's Sound												
105. Conducting and Improvising Game	●				●		●					
106. Frolicking Frogs and Slithering Snakes		●										
107. Conducting Crescendos and Diminuendos					●		●					
108. Making up Rhythms with Picture Cards		●		●								
109. Faster and Slower			●									
110. Trains in Music												

Attainment Target 2: Listening and appraising

The development of the ability to listen to and appraise music, including knowledge of musical history, our diverse musical heritage, and a variety of other musical traditions.

End of Key Stage statements	By the end of key stage 1, pupils should be able to: a) listen attentively and respond to short pieces of music from different times and cultures and in different styles, showing an awareness of differences and similarities.											b) talk in simple but appropriate terms about sounds and music they have made, listened to, performed or composed.
ACTIVITY / PROGRAMMES OF STUDY — Pupils should:	i) learn to listen with care and concentration to their own and others' music, and make broad distinctions within the main musical elements of: **pitch** – high/low	**duration** – pulse; rhythm; long/short sounds	**pace** – fast/slow	**timbre** – quality of sound	**texture** – one sound/several sounds	**dynamics** – loud/quiet	**structure** – pattern; phrasing; repetition/contrast	**silence**	ii) listen to, discover, make, compare and talk about everyday sounds of all kinds.	iii) respond to the musical elements, character and mood of a piece of music, by means of movement, dance, or other forms of expression.	iv) listen to and talk about a variety of live and recorded music exhibiting contrasts of style, including works by well-known composers and performers as well as their own and others' compositions and improvisations.	v) discuss how sounds and rhythms are used in music to achieve particular effects, and learn to recognise some different characteristics in music from different times and places
89. Music About Clocks										●		●
90. Coming Nearer and Moving Away						●				●		
91. Sounds Approaching and Departing						●						●
92. First and Last Note Pitch Game	●											
93. Picture Rhythms with Silent Gestures												
94. Am I Moing Towards You or Am I Moving Away?										●		
95. Picture Notation Without Words												
96. Hunt the Thimble						●				●		
97. Smooth Snakes										●		
98. Let's Make a Crescendo						●						
99. Volume Listening Activity						●						
100. Leaping Frogs										●		
101. 'Smooth' and 'Leaping' Melodies	●									●		●
102. Let's Make a Diminuendo												
103. Steps and Leaps	●					●				●		
104. Spot the Tune From It's Sound	✕	●										
105. Conducting and Improvising Game						●						●
106. Frolicking Frogs and Slithering Snakes	●											
107. Conducting Crescendos and Diminuendos					●	●	●					●
108. Making up Rhythms with Picture Cards	✕											
109. Faster and Slower										●		
110. Trains in Music			●									●

Attainment Target 1: Performing and composing

The development of the ability to perform and compose music with understanding.

End of Key Stage statements / PROGRAMMES OF STUDY — ACTIVITY	a) perform simple rhythmic and melodic patterns by ear and from symbols.		b) sing in a group and play simple instruments demonstrating some control of the sounds made.					c) investigate, choose and combine sounds to produce simple compositions.			d) record their own compositions and communicate them to others.	
Pupils should:	i) memorise and internalise short musical patterns and simple songs, and imitate and recall simple rhythms and melodies.	ii) read simple signs and symbols and perform from them.	iii) sing a variety of simple unison songs with some control of breathing, dynamics and pitch.	iv) develop the technical skills needed to control the sounds of a range of tuned and untuned instruments, through playing simple pieces and accompaniments.	v) practise and rehearse, responding to direction.	vi) share their music-making, presenting their performances effectively to different audiences, for different purposes, and in a number of places with different acoustics.	vii) take part in simple vocal and instrumental improvisations, compositions and arrangements.	viii) explore and use a range of sound sources including their voices, bodies, sounds from the environment and instruments, tuned and untuned.	ix) create, select and organise sounds in response to different stimuli.	x) communicate simple musical ideas.	xi) use and understand simple signs and symbols for musical sounds when composing.	xii) record their own compositions.
111. Forte, Piano, Crescendo and Diminuendo		●			●		●	●			●	
112. Rhythmic Patterns in More Than One Part		●			●							
113. Two Part Inventions												
114. Tuneful Pictures		●										
115. Playing as a Band		●		●		●						
116. Composing Fast and Slow Sounds								●	●	●		
117. Playing as a Band 2		●		●								
118. Composing Using Loud and Soft Sounds								●	●			
119. Identifying Like and Unlike Phrases			●									
120. Instrumental and Vocal Performance		●	●	●		●	●		●		●	

Attainment Target 2: Listening and appraising

The development of the ability to listen to and appraise music, including knowledge of musical history, our diverse musical heritage, and a variety of other musical traditions.

End of Key Stage statements	By the end of key stage 1, pupils should be able to: a) listen attentively and respond to short pieces of music from different times and cultures and in different styles, showing an awareness of differences and similarities.											b) talk in simple but appropriate terms about sounds and music they have made, listened to, performed or composed.
PROGRAMMES OF STUDY / ACTIVITY	Pupils should: i) learn to listen with care and concentration to their own and others' music, and make broad distinctions within the main musical elements of: pitch – high/low	duration – pulse; rhythm; long/short sounds	pace – fast/slow	timbre – quality of sound	texture – one sound/several sounds	dynamics – loud/quiet	structure – pattern; phrasing; repetition/contrast	silence	ii) listen to, discover, make, compare and talk about everyday sounds of all kinds.	iii) respond to the musical elements, character and mood of a piece of music, by means of movement, dance, or other forms of expression.	iv) listen to and talk about a variety of live and recorded music exhibiting contrasts of style, including works by well-known composers and performers as well as their own and others' compositions and improvisations.	v) discuss how sounds and rhythms are used in music to achieve particular effects, and learn to recognise some different characteristics in music from different times and places
111. Forte, Piano, Crescendo and Diminuendo												
112. Rhythmic Patterns in More Than One Part												
113. Two Part Inventions	●	●			●							●
114. Tuneful Pictures	●											
115. Playing as a Band												
116. Composing Fast and Slow Sounds			●								●	
117. Playing as a Band 2												
118. Composing Using Loud and Soft Sounds				●			●					
119. Identifying Like and Unlike Phrases							●					
120. Instrumental and Vocal Performance							●					

PERFORMING, LISTENING AND COMPOSING

THE TEACHING OF SINGING ▶

Why should we teach singing?

Since it is actually part of us, the voice is the most intimately controllable of instruments and allows for musical involvement of the most personal kind. Singing is, therefore, likely to have a profound effect on our musical development.

Singing allows us to extend the use of the voice, making it into an expressive instrument. This is likely to have a beneficial effect on our use of the voice in everyday situations and not just in a musical context.

The voice is the most easily portable and cheapest of instruments.

The National Curriculum and singing

Singing in the classroom has declined over the last twenty years. 'Serious' music making has often been equated with instrumental performance, and vocal work has been relegated to second place. The two aspects of music are, in fact, complementary and should not be regarded as alternative options. This is clearly emphasised in National Curriculum documentation.

How can I teach singing if I haven't got a voice?

It is surprising how many teachers seem to think that unless they have a voice like Pavarotti or Kiri Te Kanawa, they have no right to describe themselves as singers and therefore never perform to their pupils. Few of us would expect to be invited to read 'Book at Bedtime' on the radio but we happily read stories to our classes. In the same way, we do not mind admitting to playing football or tennis although we would never make a Gazza or Agassi. So why should singing be any different?

Singing is a practical activity. The only way to learn how to do it is to make practical experiments. Use your voice as often as possible. Do not be put off by other people's comments and draw comfort from the tremendous support that young children give their teachers.

How can I teach singing when I can't play the piano?

You do not have to use it! Too often, teachers overestimate the importance and usefulness of the piano in music lessons. This instrument has many practical disadvantages when teaching singing:

A note on the piano, once played, quickly dies away. This constant falling off of the sound is quite different from the effect which we should be striving for in singing. A melody played on the piano is not, therefore, a particularly good example for pupils to imitate.

Unless you are prepared to sing, your pupils will never have a go

The volume of sound produced by the piano often makes it difficult for a teacher to gain an accurate notion of how the class is performing. It is all too easy to convince oneself that the louder one plays, the louder the class is singing. This is rarely the case. Confident in the knowledge that the teacher is deafened by their own playing, many children quickly become very competent mime artists.

There is a great danger of becoming anchored behind a piano and of creating a 'no-man's land' between the teacher and the pupils.

Unless a teacher is confident and knows a piece extremely well, there is a danger that the position of the fingers on the keyboard becomes totally absorbing, at the expense of eye contact and close rapport with the class.

Points to bear in mind if you do use the piano

Position the piano so that you can see the class and maintain contact with them. Some teachers like to face their classes and to stand behind the piano while playing. Others prefer to place the piano at an oblique angle and to play in a sitting position. Try both approaches and decide which suits you best. Whichever approach you take, do not stay anchored to the instrument. Move around your class so that you can hear them and they can hear you.

Make sure that you can play the music accurately without having to fumble for the notes.

Practise playing songs in a variety of keys so that you can adapt to voices of varying ranges.

Try to balance accompanied work with unaccompanied singing.

Advantages of the guitar in the classroom

This instrument enables you to be near your pupils and to maintain close contact with them when performing.

Since it is an ideal accompanying instrument, there is little danger of it overpowering your own voice when singing.

As it is so portable, there is no reason for you to stay in one spot. When helping small groups or individuals in various parts of the room, you can take the instrument up to them and give any required support without attracting the attention of the rest of the class.

Through the use of the capo, you can transpose a tune into keys which suit the children's voices.

If you do not play the piano or guitar, sing unaccompanied

Unaccompanied singing should be the basis and central focus of all singing lessons, even when the teacher is an accomplished instrumentalist. Working without accompaniment helps develop accuracy of pitch and a high degree of listening – both of which are essential for any musician.

A policy of 'Do as I say and not as I do' will never succeed with singing

HOW TO TEACH A SONG

Whatever your reasons for teaching a song to your pupils, whether it is to develop their vocal skills, to help them learn to read music notation, to extend their knowledge of their culture, or simply to enable them to have an enjoyable experience, be clear in your mind about what you are trying to achieve. Your goals will influence both the type of song that you teach and how you set about presenting it to your class.

Teaching a song by rote

Much of your teaching of singing will need to be done by rote. One possible approach to this is detailed below. It is not meant to be followed slavishly, but it can be a useful starting point and has been well tried by a wide range of teachers (particularly teachers who regard themselves as 'non-specialists').

Stage I: Introduce the song by means of a picture, a story or a related event or activity. Presenting a song 'out of the blue' can be very confusing for children, so this is an essential stage. On the other hand, do not let the preamble cause an unnecessary delay in the presentation of the song.

Stage II: Sing the entire song to the children, making it as interesting as possible. If the song tells a story then make sure that you involve the children in it, just as you would if you were speaking it. Use interesting facial expressions and gestures if necessary. Always make sure that you are looking at them and communicating with them. By doing this, you will bring your existing skills to bear on a less familiar area and help to build your own confidence.

Stage III: Lead a brief discussion of the words, drawing attention to any particular aspect of the text that you might want to emphasise, e.g. the sequence of numerals in a counting song.

Stage IV: Sing the song to the class again. As with other areas of the curriculum, children (especially young children) need and enjoy repetition.

Stage V: a) Sing the first line of the song, more than once if necessary. From the outset, get the children used to preparing for their performance by beating several introductory beats and counting regularly 1–2 or 1–2–3 or 1–2–3–4 at the speed at which the rhyme or song is to be performed. You will probably find that the children will eventually count in with you. This should not be discouraged. At a later stage, ask them to 'think' introductory beats or mark them silently with movements. The appropriate count is indicated for each song in the book, as is the chime bar which you can use to give yourself and the children the appropriate starting note.

b) Sing the first note, count the class in on that note and ask the children to sing the first line. Repeat this several times if necessary.

Stage VI: Sing the second line a few times and ask the children to sing it back to you, several times if necessary. Remember that, at each stage, you will need to give the first note and count the class in.

Stage VII: The first two lines are now combined, first by you and then by the children.

Stage VIII: Gradually, through a series of teacher demonstrations and pupil imitations, the lines are built up into the whole song. You could use a variety of sequences for this, e.g.: A three-line verse might be presented in this order: Line A, Line B, Line C, Lines B and C, Lines A to C. A six-line song might be presented like this: A, B, AB, CD, ABCD, EF, G, EFG, whole verse. When you have gained more confidence, experiment with other sequences.

Disguising the repetition

By presenting a song in the ways described, you are making it easier for the children to grasp. With so much repetition, however, it would be very easy for the lesson to become monotonous. Ways to disguise the repetitions are listed below:

- Vary the volume of the repetitions – sing them loudly sometimes and softly at other times
- Let the music get louder or softer, where appropriate
- Ask groups of children to sing, rather than the whole class
- Invite individuals to sing. This is far easier than teachers often imagine. A child who is complimented for his or her singing in the group will be more than ready to take up the invitation to sing alone. Praising

that child and then inviting others to sing a solo usually leads to too many rather than too few volunteers
- Ask the children who come to school by bus to sing together
- With children who have learnt when their birthdays are, ask all those with birthdays in a specific month or group of months to sing together
- Ask all the children on the blue table, the orange table, the red table, etc. to sing together
- Intersperse the repetitions with short anecdotes or jokes
- Dispense with the words occasionally and ask the children to hum or sing to one syllable such as 'coo'.

This list is by no means exhaustive but should serve to illustrate the point that essential repetition need not necessarily be boring.

Support your children when they sing

Accept their work so long as they have done their best, but do not be content with a standard of work which can be made better. Strive to improve it. This is a delicate balancing exercise which is as important in music as in any other area of the curriculum.

Keep the lesson lively

Maintain a lively pace in the lesson. Music making is a physical activity and should be as lively and exciting as a well-run games lesson.

Introducing a new song

Learning uses up energy. It is best, therefore, to introduce a new song at the beginning of a lesson. Do not try to teach long songs, in their entirety, in one lesson. Pushing children beyond their attention span is counter-productive. Breaks between learning can actually speed up the overall process.

IMPROVING YOUR CHILDREN'S PERFORMANCE ▷

When children have performed a song or a section of it, do not be too hasty in pointing out faults. Praise them instead, wherever possible, for their 'feel' of the song and for their surmounting of the various difficulties in it. Only then should you begin to suggest how their singing could be improved. Strategies which you may wish to use to improve aspects of your children's performance are listed below. It is not advisable to make more than two or three of these 'corrections' at a time and all the approaches to a particular problem cannot be implemented in one lesson. Adapt these approaches to suit your particular circumstances.

Improving the volume of the singing

When children are not used to singing, or when it has been approached half-heartedly, they tend to produce a very quiet sound. Even classes which sing regularly will lapse from time to time. Without at least a moderately

loud sound, the children will never gain much confidence and it will be difficult to try to remedy other problems, such as unclear diction or inappropriate phrasing. One possible way to improve the volume of singing is this:

i. Take a line of the song
ii. Divide your class into groups of four or five children
iii. Sing the line to the children a few times and then ask the first group to sing it back to you
iv. Repeat the process with the next group
v. Ask both groups to sing together after you have demonstrated to them again
vi. Continue the process around the class in this sequence:
   a. teacher demonstration
   b. demonstration by a specific group
   c. performance by all groups who have performed up to that point.

Encourage your children to produce a confident volume of sound

Be very encouraging with each group and compliment them on their work unless, of course, they are deliberately making little effort.

Experience with large numbers of children over a wide age range would suggest that, by the time the whole class is singing, the volume will have increased considerably.

Remember that the object of this exercise is to produce a confident volume of sound, not to get the class to the point where all the children are shouting in competition with each other.

Improving children's stance when singing

'Hold your heads up' is an exhortation often heard during singing activities. It is not, however, a particularly useful one. If the head is held too high, the throat becomes constricted and leads to the production of a very 'contorted' sound. Any 'high' notes will also seem particularly difficult to children with their heads at this angle, since they will have the impression that all the notes are soaring way out of reach above them. The children will produce a better sound, and find it easier to sing higher notes, if they incline their heads slightly forward and look towards a point on the floor about six to ten feet ahead of them. (A strategically placed object can work wonders to keep a child's attention on one spot.)

Singing relies on effective breathing. This cannot be achieved when the diaphragm is contorted as, for example, when a child is slouching over a desk or sitting slumped in a chair. If you tried to run with your body bent double, you would soon run out of breath. The same holds true if you try to sing in such a position. Therefore do not be afraid to ask your children to stand when singing. We expect children to stand in PE and games lessons and there is no reason why we should not do the same in a music session. It is important, of course, to vary the activities so that the children are not standing too long or unnecessarily. As in any other

aspect of your work, ring the changes and make sure that there is plenty of variety.

You might occasionally ask the children to sit with their backs straight. Unfortunately they will tend to forget, with the result that either the notion of a good posture is gradually abandoned or you have to keep nagging at them, to the boredom and frustration of all concerned. Standing achieves the desired end with far less fuss.

Standing well improves singing

Improving diction

If the words of a song are to be audible to a listener, the consonants in them need to be emphasised. There are several simple strategies which can help children to do this, e.g.

i. Ask the children to lip-read silent messages sent by yourself. Then arrange for pairs of children to communicate with each other in this way. This will encourage them to exaggerate their mouth gestures.

ii. Maintaining these exaggerated mouth gestures, the children now whisper a message or line of a song, pronouncing only the consonants. The vowels should not produce any sound at all. To make sure, ask the children to place their hands on their throats. If there is any vibration while the vowels are being mouthed, the children will need to correct themselves.

iii. These activities can again be made into a game, e.g.:
   a. by sending messages around the class in 'consonant whispers'
   b. by asking a child to listen behind a screen or outside a door to hear whether a message whispered by the class can be understood.

Remember that these games and exercises are a means to an end and not an end in themselves. Therefore make sure that the techniques being developed are applied at each stage to sung as well as spoken activities.

Consonant whispers

Quite often when children come to apply these techniques to singing, they will over-exaggerate them. Do not let this worry you. The exaggeration can be toned down by you, or the children will do it for themselves.

Improving phrasing

Too often the performance of a song is spoiled by insufficient attention to phrasing. Thus, for example, a class will sing: 'The fox went out (breath) one chilly night' instead of 'The fox went out one chilly night' (breath).

A singer should try, as far as possible, to breathe at the natural breaks in sentences rather than cutting across the punctuation of a line. Where two lines follow on from one another, the link should be maintained. For example, you should sing 'Good King Wenceslas looked out on the feast of Stephen', not 'Good King Wenceslas looked out (breath) on the feast of Stephen'. Careful attention to these simple points can improve the quality of a performance considerably.

One of the main reasons for unnecessary and inappropriate breaks in a line is that children run out of breath. To combat this, try to help them to breathe more efficiently.

Improving breathing

Many tomes have been devoted to this subject. The most important points to remember are these:

i.   When breathing in, fill the lower part of the lungs first, then the upper part. This is helped by placing a hand on the tummy, just below the rib cage and pushing it out with breath, before pushing out the upper part of the chest. This should be done without raising the shoulders.
ii. When breathing out, reverse the process, with the upper lungs being emptied first.
iii. Children often breathe out too quickly. One way to help them overcome this is to let them breathe on to a mirror and keep it misted up as they exhale.

With increasing experience and confidence, you will no doubt discover further techniques to help improve your children's work. Once again, remember that the approaches described above should not all be used at once and do not try to tackle too many problems in one go. Be alert though, whenever you are singing, to ways in which you can develop the work in future lessons.

WORKING WITH INSTRUMENTS

As has already been seen, the National Curriculum Attainment Targets and Programmes of Study place considerable emphasis on giving children the opportunity to work with tuned (pitched) and untuned (unpitched) instruments. This section will give the inexperienced musician some guidance on the types of instruments which fall into these categories and how they might be approached. Further help on using instruments is contained within the individual activities.

From the time they enter school, children should have access to a wide range of instruments which are well made, attractive to hold, look at, listen to and play,

and of an appropriate size for small hands. These instruments need to be readily accessible, so that children can experiment with them and get to know them well.

Instruments inevitably make a noise. There is a difference, however, between controlled noise and chaos. In a PE, games or dance lesson, children are taught when to start, stop, put the equipment down, experiment with ideas, observe each other and observe the teacher. The same approaches are equally applicable to working with instruments and to several other aspects of music making.

As with any other equipment, musical instruments

need to be handled with care. This can, however, be taken to extremes. A child who is only ever allowed free access to an old, unattractive instrument while the 'best' ones are confined to 'the music lesson' can be forgiven for losing interest.

Like any other equipment, musical instruments do wear out. Therefore, every school should have a policy of investment and replacement for musical instruments.

What types of instruments should you use?

A basic stock of classroom instruments should contain a variety of wooden and metal, untuned (unpitched) and tuned (pitched) instruments. It is better to invest in one or two examples of several types of instruments than in trying to give every child an example of one specific instrument.

The types of instruments useful at Key Stage 1 (with brief details of how they might be played) are listed below. Remember not to confine yourself or your pupils to one way of performing. Composers are always looking for ways to extend the range of sounds available to them. This process of investigation should begin at the school level and should not be arrested by an over concern with confining children to one 'conventional' way of playing a particular instrument.

UNTUNED (UNPITCHED) PERCUSSION ▶

Afuchie (or cabasa)

This is usually played by rotating the beads against the central metal cylinder, producing a grating sound. Alternatively, it can be played by shaking it.

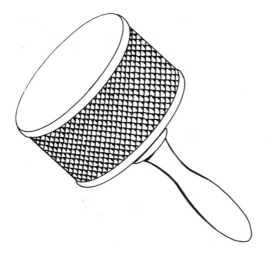

Cabasa (or shekere)

This is made of a dried gourd shell, strung with a loose mesh of seeds or beads. Very young children might find that, even with a small version, the handle is difficult to hold. By the time they reach year two, however, most children should be able to manipulate this instrument quite successfully.

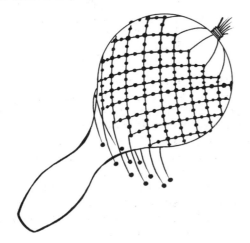

Castanets

Castanets are played by holding them between the thumb and the first three fingers and closing them together to create a clicking sound. The easiest type for infant children to handle are those which have a tight elasticated joint at the base. Other types, held together by string, can be almost impossible for some small children to manage.

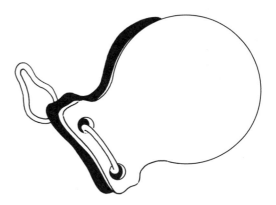

Hand held castanets are probably better for younger children. These can be played in a variety of ways, e.g. by holding the handle in one hand and flicking it forward so that the two clappers click against the central handle. Or they could be held in one hand and struck against the thigh or the palm of the other hand.

6

Claves (rhythm sticks)

These are played by striking one against the other.

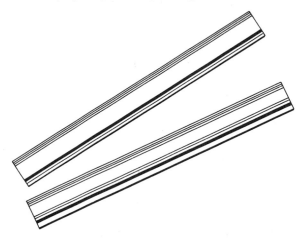

Cymbals

These can be played by clashing them together or by holding one of them by the handle, so that it is parallel to the floor, and striking it with a beater.

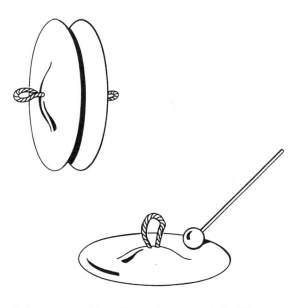

It is also possible to have finger cymbals. These come in pairs and are attached to finger and thumb and struck together. Young children and those with very thin fingers can find these very difficult to play.

Finger cymbals

Indian bells consist of a pair of small cymbals suspended at both ends of the same piece of string. They are played by striking one against the other.

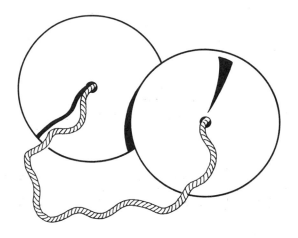

Indian bells

Drums

A wide variety of drums are available. Children should be given access to several types and sizes, e.g. bongo drums, hand drums. They are played by tapping with the hand or striking with a beater.

Guiro (resi-resi, scraper or rasp)

This consists of a tube with a serrated edge, along which a scraper is drawn to produce a rasping sound. Guiros come in several sizes and shapes, including cylindrical shapes and fish shapes The smaller fish-shaped guiros are probably easiest for infants to hold because of the handle provided by the fish's tale.

Guiros are made of a variety of materials, including metal and wood. Metal guiros often have more than one type of serrated surface, so that it is possible to produce a greater variety of sounds on them.

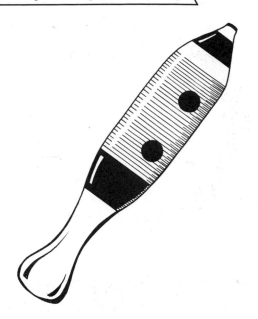

either hand and shaking them alternately. Small children find one maraca easier to manage. This can be played by holding it in one hand and tapping it against the palm of the other hand.

Rattles

These come in many forms and are made from a variety of materials – plastic, wood and cane.

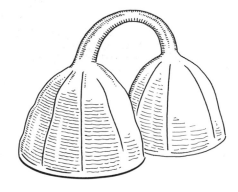

Jingle bells

These come in many forms, with or without handles.

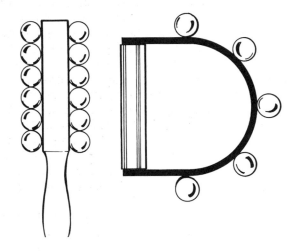

Shakers

A common and durable shaker useful in the classroom is one made from a lightweight metal tube.

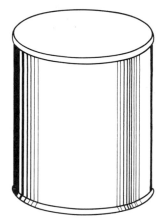

Maracas

Maracas are a variety of rattle. Originally made from gourds, they now come in a variety of materials, including plastic and wood. They are usually sold in pairs. Ideally they should be played by holding one in

Tambour

A tambour is a shallow drum. It looks rather like a tambourine without its jingles. Like a drum, it can be played with the hands or with beaters.

Tambourine

Tambourines come in several varieties: with a skin, without a skin and in interesting shapes like the half-moon tambourine.

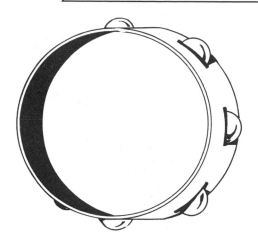

TUNED (PITCHED) INSTRUMENTS

Agogo

An agogo consists of two hollow tubes of different sizes mounted on a handle. The two tubes are struck with a beater to produce two notes: a higher and a lower pitched one. The tubes on wooden agogos often have serrated sides so that they can double as guiros (see above).

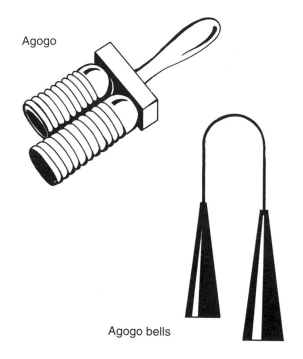

Agogo

Agogo bells

There are also metal versions known as agogo bells or metal agogos. In some instances, metal agogos can have more than two bells.

Beaters

Tuned percussion instruments are usually played with beaters. These will vary in terms of the size of the head, the length of the stick and the hardness of the material from which the head is made. Xylophones, glockenspiels and metallophones usually come with a pair of beaters suitable for use with those specific instruments. You can, however, produce a wide range of effects from

one instrument by varying the type of beater used. Generally speaking, the harder the beater head, the more piercing the sound produced on the instrument.

It is advisable to buy extra sets of beaters to cover losses and to give the children a wider range of possibilities for experimenting. To minimise loss or breakages, and to avoid unnecessary expenditure, make sure that you have a clear system for distributing and collecting beaters when using them in the classroom.

A single beater would be appropriate for use with a single chime bar and also on occasion with glockenspiels, xylophones and metallophones. As the children get older and more adept at manipulating the sticks, encourage them to use a pair of beaters at a time. This allows for the playing of more than one note simultaneously (a chord) and makes faster music easier to play.

At an even later stage in their development, children could be encouraged to hold more than one beater in one hand. This, however, will be a rare feat for children at Key Stage 1.

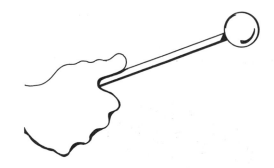

Encourage the children to hold the beaters as shown in the illustration above and to make the beater bounce on the bar of the instrument so that it produces a clear note. This is not to say that they should not also be given the chance to experiment with other ways of making a sound. If, for example, a child wants to produce a very short note when making up music on a glockenspiel, he or she may prefer to strike the bar and keep the beater on it rather than letting it bounce.

Cow bells

Unlike alpine cow bells, percussion cow bells do not have clappers. Instead the sound is produced by striking them on the outer surface with a beater. Different sized cow bells produce different pitched sounds. The larger the cow bell, the lower the sound.

Individual cow bells can be held in the hand, although this would be difficult for the average infant. Alternatively, they can be mounted on a particular type of stand specially produced for the purpose.

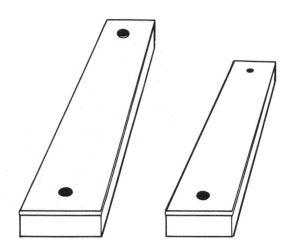

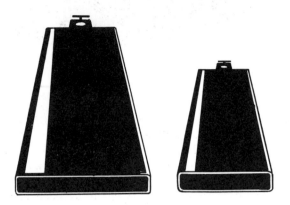

Temple blocks

These are hollow wooden instruments which sound when struck on the outer surface. Like cow bells, they come in different sizes and are mounted on a stand.

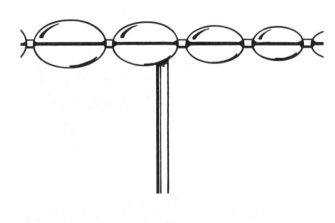

Chime bar

A chime bar consists of a hollow box or tube to which is attached a metal bar tuned to a particular pitch. The pitch of the note is usually stamped on the surface of the bar. It is possible to have chime bars covering a wide range of pitches. Each note is a separate instrument, although they can be grouped together to make scales of notes. A chime bar is usually played by being struck with a beater. The sound will keep vibrating for a considerable time after being struck. It can however be dampened by putting a finger on the surface as soon as it has been struck.

Glockenspiel

A glockenspiel consists of a long open box divided into resonance chambers. Balanced across the upper edges of the box are nickel-plated steel bars of varying sizes. These are sounded by being struck with beaters. As with chime bars, the larger the bar on a glockenspiel, the lower the pitch of the note it produces.

Conventionally a glockenspiel is arranged so that the largest and lowest sounding bar is on the extreme left as the player looks at the instrument. The bars then become progressively smaller and progressively higher in pitch as their position moves to the right of the instrument. The smallest bar (and therefore the highest pitched note) is the one at the far right of the instrument.

A *diatonic* glockenspiel is one which has the notes CDEFGABCDEFGA i.e. notes which correspond in pitch to the white notes on a piano.

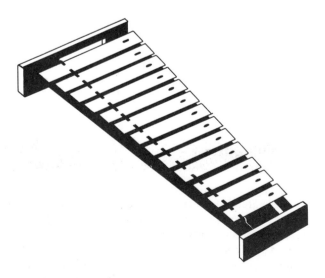

A soprano diatonic glockenspiel

A *chromatic* glockenspiel has the above notes plus a second row of notes which correspond in pitch to the black notes on the piano.

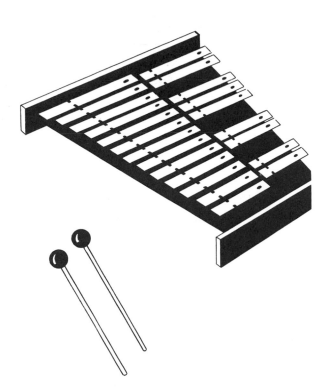

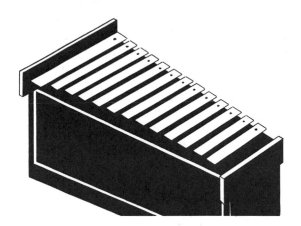

A bass diatonic metallophone

Xylophone

A xylophone is constructed on the same principle as the glockenspiel and metallophone. The bars on the xylophone, however, are made of wood, usually rosewood. It is also played with beaters, although the sound vibrates for a shorter period than in the case of the other two instruments. Xylophones can be diatonic or chromatic and are again arranged so that notes become higher from left to right. There are three types of xylophone: soprano, alto and bass, each larger and of a lower pitch range than the preceding one.

An alto chromatic glockenspiel

The bars on most glockenspiels can be removed. This can be very useful if you are only wanting to focus on one or two sounds.

There are two types of glockenspiel: soprano and alto. The soprano has a smaller overall size and therefore has a higher pitch range than the alto glockenspiel.

Metallophone

A metallophone is constructed on the same principles as a glockenspiel, except that the bars are made of aluminium alloy. Metallophones are arranged and played in the same way as glockenspiels and can be of a diatonic or chromatic type. There are three types of metallophone: soprano (highest pitch range); alto (medium pitch range); bass (lowest pitch range). As before, the smaller the overall size of the instrument, the higher its pitch range. The vibration of notes on a metallophone lasts longer than those on the glockenspiel.

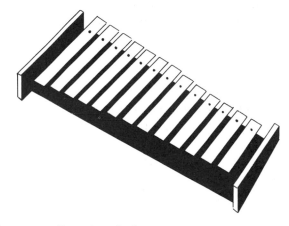

A soprano diatonic xylophone

THE IMPORTANCE OF LISTENING

Listening is fundamental to any musical activity whether it be: tuning an instrument, playing a scale evenly, rehearsing and practising a piece, improvising, composing, or presenting a performance. It also includes, of course, attending to performances by other people in live or recorded form. We need to be aware, however, of certain problems and pitfalls where this last type of activity is concerned.

Disadvantages of an information-based approach

There is a great danger of music becoming 'swamped in a welter of information about music, about composers, about instruments' (Salaman, W., *Living School Music,*

Cambridge University Press, 1982). This is particularly true where lessons devoted to listening to recorded performances are concerned. The disadvantage of such an approach is that it often detracts from, or becomes a substitute for, that direct live experience which is essential in music.

'Information may possibly, in some roundabout way, motivate us to listen more attentively, but it will not in itself aid us in our perception of music. There is nothing that can be said that will equal the direct experience of the sound' (Paynter, J., *Music in the Secondary School Curriculum,* Cambridge University Press, 1982).

11

Disadvantages of recorded music

Listening to music on record or tape is a very difficult activity and in many ways an unnatural one. If you go to any kind of concert, you do not usually sit there with your eyes closed, listening only to the sound. You watch the performers and audience and these visual stimuli can add to the interest and often help concentration and understanding.

You, as the teacher, have the advantage of knowing the music and of having experienced live performances as a listener or singer or instrumentalist. Therefore you are able, through experience and imagination, to compensate for the missing 'live' musical elements. This is unlikely to be true of a class of young children.

Active exploration of music

It is important, therefore, that children's listening grows from an active exploration of music. Children who have tried to make up a story through their compositions are likely to be far more interested and to know what to listen for when they come to hear a musical story produced by a professional composer. 'Their own activity in putting sounds together, or in taking decisions about points of interpretation or style of presentation, technically simple though it may be, will provide the all important bridge between the reality of musical experience and the recorded sound.' (Paynter, 1982).

'Those who have made up their own music are usually more discerning when they hear the music of others' (DES, 1985).

Active, task-oriented listening

Whatever the style of the music children listen to, they are likely to gain far more if they are asked to listen to something specific. If children are set few, or no tasks, they will achieve little or nothing and, at best, be no more than passive witnesses of a wash of meaningless sound.

A few examples of ways to focus children's listening are listed below. The list is not definitive but intended to help prompt your own ideas.

- Distinguishing between loud and soft, fast and slow, high and low sounds in the music.
- Deciding whether the music runs, skips, walks or gallops.
- Identifying musical phrases (see glossary) and accents (see glossary).
- Identifying a well-known tune in the context of a larger work.
- Identifying a particular melodic progression when it is used for an ostinato (see glossary), for example.
- Identifying a rhythmic pattern (see glossary), already performed live, when it appears, or reappears, in a composed work.
- Identifying different timbres (see glossary) of instruments, voices, or combinations of these.
- Listening to the way a melody is used. Is it pitched high or low, for example? Does it move smoothly or is it played staccato (see glossary)? Does the mood of the melody change during successive appearances? If so, what causes it to change?
- Listening for recurrences of sections of music, i.e. attending to formal patterns.
- Where 'programme' music (i.e. descriptive music, or music which 'tells a story') is concerned, identifying when a particular event occurs. Remember that a great deal of the music played to young children tends to fall into this category. There is a danger, however, that with this type of music, peripheral elements become the focus of attention rather than the music itself. It is not so much the story itself but how it is told that is important. Focusing on the latter leads us into the music itself.

What types of music should the children listen to?

It is quite clear from the National Curriculum Attainment Targets and Programmes of Study that

Exploring music

12

children should be exposed to as wide a range of musical styles as possible. You might have a particular liking for one type of music. Convey your enthusiasm to your pupils by all means, but do not allow your own preferences to dominate, since this could limit your pupils' and your own experiences.

Resources for listening

The best way to build up a resource is to listen to a vast range of music. The references in this book are meant as no more than a starting point for such exploration. Simply relying on a narrow range of well-known works 'appropriate' for school will not do. Try to extend your own and your pupils' experiences as much as possible. Do not dismiss a particular piece of music because you think that the children will find it strange or obscure. Remember that their preferences and prejudices have not yet been formed to the same extent as your own and they might actually help you hear more in a piece than you at first expected. At various stages in this book, you will find suggestions for listening, together with advice on the types of elements to which the children's attention could be drawn in a specific piece of music.

COMPOSING ▶

Composing is probably the area of the music curriculum which has struck the greatest fear into the hearts of primary school teachers, regardless of whether they have had much experience of music teaching or not. As with singing, teachers often imagine that, unless they themselves are outstanding at this activity, they cannot begin to present it to their pupils. How many teachers who pursue creative writing activities with their pupils have ever written a publishable poem or novel? How many teachers who pursue art with a class have ever exhibited a painting?

In the area of creative writing and art, teachers have long realised that the most important thing is to provide opportunities for children to investigate, experiment and try out ideas. The results of such endeavours are not to be compared with publicly acclaimed works but are to be viewed in relation to the emerging skills of the pupils at that particular age or stage of development.

The same should hold true for music. A child's composition at infant level might not be a symphony but, if it reflects an attempt to make a pattern out of a range of sounds which the child has tried out, then it could be the first step on the journey to creating one.

As teachers gain more experience of helping children 'mess about with sounds' they will, as they have with visual arts and improvised drama, begin to build a set of expectations, be more realistic in their approach and, one hopes, become more confident about it.

Meanwhile, in this book for Key Stage 1, the emphasis will be on providing basic guidelines to enable both teacher and pupils to work together on finding ways of experimenting and creating in sound.

Children composing

MUSIC ACTIVITIES FOR KEY STAGE 1

STARTING POINTS

Choosing a starting point for working with infants is not easy because of the wide variations in their experiences. Some will have encountered a tremendous amount of music at home, in playgroups or in nursery classes. Others will not have had such advantages. Some will have a sizeable repertoire of nursery rhymes and songs. Others will have to be provided with such a repertoire from scratch. This difference in experience should also be borne in mind at other stages of teaching music. Too often schools are tempted to combine classes together for music. This makes the whole issue of coverage very difficult since the range of experience is then increased, whilst the opportunities for adressing the differences positively are considerably reduced.

This book provides one possible starting point. But it will be up to the teacher to adapt it to suit the particular needs of her class.

Finger rhymes
Finger rhymes and nursery rhymes are an extremely important aspect of a young child's education. As well as being part of a child's cultural heritage, they are also a means of developing co-ordination, sequencing, learning about colours, counting, days of the week, months of the year and a host of other aspects of their life. They are also an important means to introduce children to concepts basic to their musical development such as high/low, fast /slow, up/down, etc.

The next few activities show how rhymes can be used as a starting point for developing musical concepts. These examples should be sufficient to trigger off further ideas, should the teacher wish to develop this approach. A particularly useful source of such rhymes is *The Oxford Nursery Rhyme Book* by Iona and Peter Opie.

Remember that children's parents or grandparents may well know rhymes which you could use to extend these ideas. If you have a parents' support group attached to your school, ask the members to help you to build up your own local repertoire of rhymes.

1. FINGER DANCE

C1

Purpose
To give children experience of moving in time to the underlying pulse of a rhyme.

Resources
Copymaster 1; cassette: side 1, track 1.

Activity
Ask the children to look at their hands. Discuss how many fingers they have on each hand. How are the fingers different? Some are fatter than others and some are longer than others. You could refer to the illustration of a hand on **Copymaster 1**. The children could also draw their own (or each other's) hands.

Recite the rhyme, 'Thumbkin says', to the children. Hold up each finger as it is mentioned and move it in time to the beat, as shown below. When you have recited the rhyme to the children once or twice, ask them to join with you in saying it and in producing the accompanying gestures. As you and the children say each verse, wag the finger referred to in time to the beat. When they have gained confidence in speaking the rhyme, teach them the tune.

THUMBKIN			
Starting note: C. Count in: 1-2-3-4 1-2-3-4			
Verse 1			
Thumbkin says, 'I'll dance'_____,			
1	2	3	4
wag	wag	wag	wag
Thumbkin says, 'I'll sing'_____			
1	2	3	4
wag	wag	wag	wag
Dance and sing, you merry little men.			
1	2	3	4
wag	wag	wag	wag
Thumbkin says, 'I'll dance and sing'.			
1	2	3	4
wag	wag	wag	wag

Make sure that the children are producing clear movements in time with the beat when performing the rhyme. Asking them to exaggerate the movements will help with this. Also ensure that they are saying the words clearly because this will make it easier for them to keep time, as they can capitalise on the inner co-ordination associated with speech.

Verse 2

Foreman says, 'I'll dance'_____,

wag   wag   wag   wag

Verse 3

Longman says, 'I'll dance'_____,

Verse 4

Ringman says, 'I'll dance'_____,

Verse 5

Littleman says, 'I'll dance'_____.

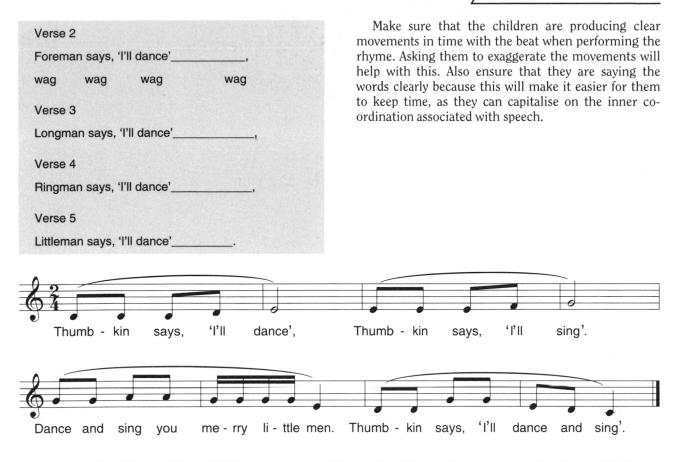

Thumb - kin says, 'I'll dance', Thumb - kin says, 'I'll sing'.

Dance and sing you me - rry li - ttle men. Thumb - kin says, 'I'll dance and sing'.

2. CLAP HANDS, CLAP HANDS

Purpose

To give children experience of feeling the underlying beat, or pulse, of a rhyme and moving in time to it.

Resources

Cassette: side 1, track 2.

Activity

This activity can be developed along the same lines as the preceding one. This time, the beat (or pulse) is marked with a hand clap.

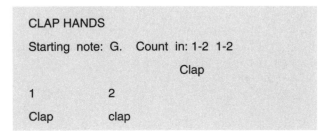

CLAP HANDS

Starting note: G.   Count in: 1-2 1-2

		Clap
1	2	
Clap	clap	

Hands	clap	hands	hip
1		2	
Clap		clap	
Hip	hoo-	ray	my
1		2	
Clap		clap	
Very	best	friend	is
1		2	
Clap		clap	
Coming	to	play	
1		2	
Clap		clap	

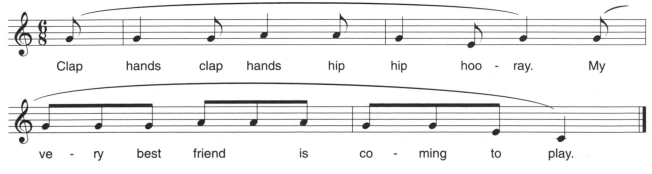

Clap   hands   clap   hands   hip   hip   hoo - ray.   My

ve - ry   best   friend   is   co - ming   to   play.

15

3. HANDY DANDY

C2,3

Purpose

To give children practice in moving in time to the underlying beat, or pulse, of a rhyme; to emphasise the notion of high and low in preparation for later work on pitch.

Resources

Copymasters 2 and 3; cassette: side 1, track 3.

Activity

Sit facing the children. Show them a small object. Pick it up and, with your hands behind your back, tell them that you are going to hide it in one fist. Bring both hands forward and then chant or sing the rhyme, marking the beat by bobbing your hands up and down on the syllables indicated. On the last line, lift one fist high in the air and point the other down towards the floor. The children then have to say which fist they think the object is in by referring to the 'high' or 'low'

one. If the child has guessed correctly he or she then sits in the centre of the circle and leads the class in the guessing game. Make sure that each child is pointing in the right direction on high and low.

HANDY DANDY	
Starting note: G. Count in: 1-2 1-2	
Handy	dandy
1	2
Bob	bob
Riddeldy	ro.
1	2
Bob	bob
What hand will you have?	
1	2
Bob	bob
Is it high or low?	
1	2
Up	down

Extension

Extend the activity using **Copymasters 2** and **3**. Make two copies of the picture of the fist and one of the bag of sweets. Mount the pictures of fists on separate cards. On the reverse side of one card, mount the picture of the bag of sweets. The game is played by holding the cards high and low or sticking them at different heights on the wall (or on the board) so that the children then have to guess which one has the sweets behind it. Producing several such sets will enable the children to play the game in pairs or groups. At a later stage, sets of three cards could be used placed at high, middle and low levels. The children would then have to use a wider vocabulary to play the guessing game.

Guessing whether the hidden object is high or low

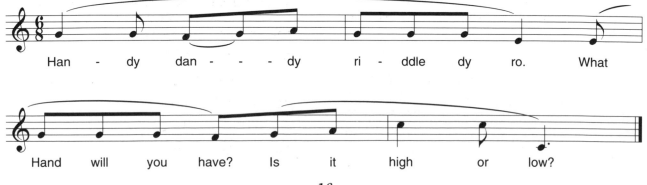

Han - dy dan - - - dy   ri - ddle dy ro.   What

Hand   will   you   have?   Is   it   high   or   low?

4. MATCHING TIMBRE GAME

C4

Purpose
To enable children to match objects on the basis of the sound they produce.

Resources
12 tin cans (six pairs) filled with a variety of things, e.g. dried peas, sand, shells, buttons, coins, marbles, Copymaster 4.

Activity
Arrange the cans randomly on a surface. Ask the children to shake one can and listen to the sound it makes. Then shake the others until they identify the container which produces the same sound. Put that pair aside and move on to the others until all six pairs have been matched.

Discuss with the children what kind of sound is made by each container. Ask them what they think might be in each one. In some instances, open the containers so that they can see what is inside producing the sound.

Extension
You can extend this activity by changing the contents of the containers, by having matching groups of three or four, by having some containers which have no matching pairs. Alternatively, the children could listen

Finding pairs of cans which produce the same sound

to each container, decide what is in it and draw the contents on **Copymaster 4.** They can then draw lines to interconnect the matching pairs.

5. HOB SHOE

C5, 6

Purpose
To give children further practice in marking the underlying beat or pulse of a rhyme through movement.

Resources
Copymasters 5 and 6; cassette: side 1, tracks 4 and 5.

Activity
Show the children the picture of a horseshoe or, better still, let them see and handle a real one. Talk about why a horse needs such shoes and how they are attached. Also talk about the blacksmith who is responsible for the process. Use **Copymasters 5** and **6** as a basis for this discussion.

Now pretend to be a blacksmith hammering the nails into the shoe. Say the rhyme as you do so, making sure that the hammer movements correspond to the beat of the rhyme. Let the children copy the movements and words.

Hob	shoe	hob_____.	
1	2	3	4
Tap	tap	tap	tap

Here a	nail and	there a	nail and
1	2	3	4
Tap	tap	tap	tap

That's	well	shod_____.	
1	2	3	4
Tap	tap	tap	tap

Another rhyme which could be used alongside, or instead of, 'Hob shoe' is 'Shoe a little horse'.

This can be presented along the same lines.

HOB SHOE			
Starting note: G. Count in: 1-2-3-4 1-2-3-4			
Hob	shoe	hob_____.	
1	2	3	4
Tap	tap	tap	tap

SHOE A LITTLE HORSE			
Starting note: G Count in: 1-2-3-4 1-2-3-4			
Shoe a	little	horse_____.	
1	2	3	4
Tap	tap	tap	tap

Shoe a	little	mare_____.	
1	2	3	4
Tap	tap	tap	tap
Let the	little	colt	go
1	2	3	4
Tap	tap	tap	tap

Bare	bare	bare_____.	
1	2	3	4
Tap	tap	tap	tap

HOB SHOE

Hob   shoe   hob.   Hob   shoe   hob.

Here a nail and there a nail and that's well shod.

SHOE A LITTLE HORSE

Shoe a li - ttle horse.   Shoe a li - ttle mare.

Let the li - ttle colt go____ bare bare bare.

6. MUSIC ABOUT HORSES

You could extend this section by playing the children a selection of pieces about horses. You could draw on the following examples or other suitable pieces with which you are more familiar: 'Knight of the Hobby Horse', from *Scenes of Childhood* by Robert Schumann; 'The Little White Donkey', by Ibert. Draw the children's attention to the way that the music imitates the movement of the horses. Play the music to them several times so that they become familiar with it. This is probably best done by setting up a listening corner where the children can go to listen in small groups and where they can talk to you or a classroom assistant about what they have heard. A listening station with several sets of earphones will be particularly useful for this type of activity. There are also many excellent opportunities here for art and movement work.

7. FAST AND SLOW

C7, 8

Purpose
To help children apply the terms 'fast' and 'slow' to real life situations, in preparation for later work on musical tempo.

Resources
Copymasters 7 and 8.

Activity
Discuss with the children the things around them which are fast and which are slow. Then introduce and discuss the pictures on the **Copymaster 7** and write 'fast' or 'slow' next to each one. Alternatively, make into cards and match with the 'fast' and 'slow' labels from **Copymaster 8**.

18

8. METRONOME GAME

C9

Purpose
To introduce children to the notion that the speed of a metronome changes according to the position of the weight on the arm; to give children practice in moving to beats of differing speeds.

Resources
A metronome with an adjustable weight; Copymaster 9.

Activity
Introduce the children to the metronome. Set the weight in the middle of the arm so that it beats at a moderate speed. Ask the children to join you in clapping in time with it. Next, adjust the weight upwards so that the arm moves more slowly. Invite the children to clap or tap in time to it again. Repeat the activity with the weight adjusted downwards so that the speed of the arm is faster.

Discuss with the children what happens when the position of the weight on the metronome is moved. (The lower the position of the weight, the faster the tick; the higher the position of the weight, the slower the tick.) Give individual children the opportunity to adjust the weight while the others move in time to the beat. The children could also chant the rhymes which they have already learnt in time to the varying speeds.

After experimenting and discussing, ask the children to decide which of the metronomes on **Copymaster 9** will go slowly and which will go quickly. Help them to test their answers out against the actual metronome.

At a later stage, when the children have had experience of moving very slowly, very quickly, moderately slowly, etc., this activity could be adapted. They can be given a number of pictures with the weights at several positions and asked to arrange them in increasing or decreasing order of speeds.

Adjusting the weight on a metronome

9. LISTENING FOR SPEED

Remind the children of the types of sounds which bees make. Invite them to imitate the sound. Now tell them that they are going to hear a piece about a musical bee. Play them a recording of 'The flight of the bumble bee' by Rimsky Korsakov or, if you feel they might not be able to concentrate on the whole piece, play a section from it.

When you have done this, discuss with them what types of sounds they have heard. Guide the discussion round to the speed of the music. Did the notes go fast or slow? (Fast.) When they have done this, play the piece or a section of it again, so that those who are uncertain of the speed will be able to hear it for themselves.

You could follow this up by playing another fast piece about bees, e.g. 'The Bees' Wedding' by Mendelssohn or the opening of *The Wasps* overture by Vaughan

Willliams. At a later point, play them a slow-moving piece, e.g. Debussy's *'Gymnopedie'* 1 or 3. Again decide whether it would be preferable to play the whole piece to them or only a section of it. As before, ask them to focus on the speed at which it is moving. (Both pieces move slowly.) You might wish to reinforce these activities further by involving the children in moving to the music. Whether you do this or not it is essential here, and at other stages, that you give the children the opportunity to listen to the pieces of music several times during the week. You could reinforce the concepts by producing a display showing a bee moving quickly and a person moving slowly and labelling these so that the children can make appropriate connections and develop concepts accordingly.

10. COBBLER, COBBLER

C10

Purpose
To give children the experience of moving in time to the underlying beat, or pulse, of a rhyme and to mark that pulse with a combination of movements; to emphasise the concept of up and down in preparation for later work on pitch.

Resources
Copymaster 10; a pair of shoes; cassette: side 1, track 6.

Activity
Remind the children that horses have to be shod and that horseshoes are made by blacksmiths. Discuss what

they themselves wear on their feet and why they need shoes. Then move on to describing the work of shoemakers or cobblers. Examine the pair of shoes on **Copymaster 10**, drawing attention to the nails and the stitching on them. Describe how a cobbler has to nail and sew the leather.

Introduce them to the song 'Cobbler, cobbler'. When they can sing this fairly accurately, sit cross-legged on the floor holding one foot in one hand so that the sole of your shoe is visible. Then, in time to the beat of the song, pretend to tap nails into the sole.

In the second half of the rhyme, mark the beat with upward and downward pointing. When this has been done a few times, invite the children to join you and to imitate the words and gestures in time to the beat. Here, and at later points, you might like to use the metronome to mark the beat while you chant or sing.

Mark the beat with a hammering action

COBBLER, COBBLER

Starting note: G.   Count in: 1-2-3-4 1-2-3-4

Cob	bler,	cob	ble	mend	my	shoe_____	.
1	2	3	4	1	2	3	4
Tap	tap	tap	tap	tap	tap	tap	tap
Get	it	done	by	half	past	two_____	.
1	2	3	4	1	2	3	4
Tap	tap	tap	tap	tap	tap	tap	tap
Stitch	it	up	and	stitch	it	down_____	,
1	2	3	4	1	2	3	4
Point up	point up	point up	point up	point up	point up	point up	point up
And	I'll	give	you	half	a	crown_____	.
1	2	3	4	1	2	3	4
Tap	tap	tap	tap	tap	tap	tap	tap

Mark the beat with upward or downward pointing

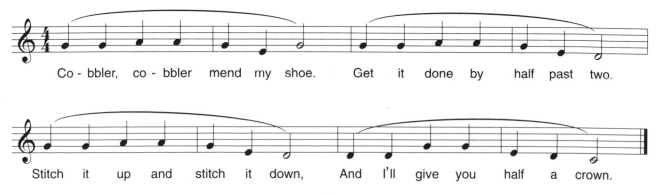

Co - bbler, co - bbler mend my shoe. Get it done by half past two.

Stitch it up and stitch it down, And I'll give you half a crown.

11. PASS THE MUSIC BAG

Purpose
To give children practice in identifying objects from the sound they make.

Resources
A bag full of objects which make a noise, e.g. keys, beads, etc.; Copymaster 11; cassette: side 1, track 7.

Activity
Teach the children the following song:

> PASS THE MUSIC BAG
>
> Starting note: F. Count in: 1-2-3-4 1-2-3-4
>
> | Pass | the | music | bag | round | and | round_____ , |
> |------|-----|-------|-----|-------|-----|--------|
> | 1 | 2 | 3 | 4 | 1 | 2 | 3 | 4 |
>
> | Round | and | round_____ | round | and | round_____ . |
> |-------|-----|------------|-------|-----|--------|
> | 1 | 2 | 3 | 4 | 1 | 2 | 3 | 4 |
>
> | Pass | the | music | bag | round | and | round_____ . |
> |------|-----|-------|-----|-------|-----|--------|
> | 1 | 2 | 3 | 4 | 1 | 2 | 3 | 4 |
>
> | Guess | what | makes | this | sound_____ ? |
> |-------|------|-------|------|--------|
> | 1 | 2 | 3 | 4 | 1 | 2 | 3 | 4 |

When they are fairly confident about singing the song, ask them to sit in a circle. Choose one child to be the starter. Give that child a bag full of objects which make a noise e.g. keys, beads, etc. As they sing the song, the children pass the bag around the circle. The child who is holding the bag when the song finishes becomes the leader. He or she reaches inside the bag and makes a noise with one of the objects inside. Another child selected by the leader then tries to guess what the object is on the basis of the sound produced. If the child guesses incorrectly then that child is 'out'. A child who guesses correctly becomes the leader and the game continues. The winner is the last child out.

Extension
Take a bag containing one or more objects and ask the children to identify what the contents are from the sound alone. This time discuss what type of sound is produced by the objects concerned (e.g. clanking, thudding, etc.) and apply a label to it. Ask the children to think of other objects which make jangling, thudding, ringing noises, etc. and make a list of them. Arrange these as sets.

Give the children a bag each. Again they have to guess the contents of the bag on the basis of the sound alone. When they have guessed what is in the bag, ask them to draw a picture of the object(s) in the empty bag on **Copymaster 11**. When they have done this, they can check to see how accurate they have been. They could also be helped to label the type of sounds produced by the objects and to colour all those which produce a particular type of sound with the same colour.

Guess what makes this sound?

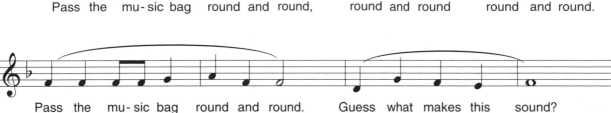

12. PAT-A-CAKE

C12

Purpose

To give the children practice in moving in time to the underlying beat (or pulse) of a song; to give children practice in accenting the strong beats in a song.

Resources

Pictures of a variety of baked foods; pictures of bakers at work – particularly kneading dough or patting pizzas; cassette: side 1, track 8; Copymaster 12.

Activity

Talk to the children about baking. Have they ever tried it? Perhaps they have helped with cooking at home or in school. Can they remember what one has to do when preparing and baking a cake? Does it take a long or a short time? What kinds of food do we bake at home? Where do the bread and cakes in the shops and the supermarkets usually come from? Show the children pictures of bakers at work. Talk about the way that bakers knead dough and how they pat bases like pizza bases into shape. Also discuss the way that cakes are decorated – sometimes with icing or pastry shapes and sometimes with patterns cut into the cake.

Teach the children the song:

PAT-A-CAKE	
Starting note: D. Count in: 1-2 1-2	
Pat-a-cake,	pat-a-cake
1	2
Baker's	man.
1	2
Bake me a	cake as
1	2
Fast as you	can.
1	2

Pat it and	prick it and
1	2
Mark it with	T.
1	2
Put it in the	oven for
1	2
Tommy and	me.
1	2

When the children are able to sing it fairly confidently, arrange them so that they stand or sit in pairs facing each other. This time on each syllable marked, the children in each pair tap each other's hands as illustrated. They might find the movements easier if they lean slightly towards each other.

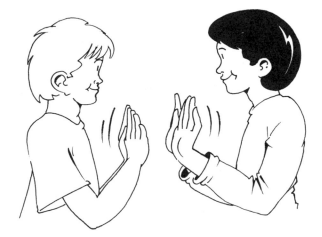

Tapping hands to emphasise the accent

To emphasise the accent arrange the children so that they are kneeling on the floor with their arms outstretched, palms facing downwards. They then

22

perform the song alternating a slap on the floor with a tap on their knees:

Pat	a	cake	pat	a	cake
Floor			knee		

Draw the children's attention to the fact that the sound which they make when they slap the floor is louder than that produced when they tap their knees. These louder beats are the accents in the song.

Extend this activity by helping each child to draw the initial letter of his or her name on the cake on **Copymaster 12**. These can be coloured in or decorated in various ways and then cut out and mounted on cards. Now, when singing the song, instead of using the name, Tommy, choose the name of a child in the class and ask that child to hold up the cake picture. Later, the children could simply be shown the letter and they have to guess which child's name is pricked in the cake.

13. LOUD AND SOFT GAME

Purpose
To help children identify loud and soft sounds; to enable the children to anticipate what volume of sound is likely to be produced by an object or a combination of objects.

Resources
A series of paired objects which can be struck together, e.g. two tennis balls, two balls of wool, two wood blocks, two identical tin lids, two cushions, two shoes, two books, etc.; Copymasters 13 and 14.

Activity
Ask a child to choose a pair of objects and to hit them together. Discuss whether the sound is soft or loud. Continue to do this with the remaining pairs, deciding in each case whether the sounds are loud or soft. After the first two pairs have been tested, ask the children to try to anticipate whether the sound about to be produced is likely to be loud or soft.

Extension
Present the children with a different set of paired objects. Ask them to anticipate the volume of the sounds which they produce. Then ask them to group all the loud sounding objects together into one circle and all the soft sounding ones into another circle. They could also draw pictures of the sets and colour them according to the volume of sound which they produce.

Ask the children to look at the pictures on **Copymaster 13** and decide, through testing and/or discussion, whether they produce loud or soft sounds. Then ask them to colour all the loud sounding objects in one colour and all the soft sounding objects in another colour. You might also use the loud and soft labels on **Copymaster 14**.

Identifying loud and soft sounds

14. LISTENING FOR VOLUME

The above activity can be extended by playing the children contrasting loud and soft music. Two suitable pieces are Debussy's 'Syrinx' and Khatchaturian's 'Dance of the Gladiators'.

In playing the first of these pieces, draw the children's attention to the fact that the music is played by a solo flute. (You could show them a picture of one, or, better still, arrange for them to see an actual one.) Also draw their attention to the fact that it is played softly for most of the time. This is in sharp contrast to the 'Dance of the Gladiators' with its loud sounds. You could also encourage the children to describe the pieces they hear in terms of whether they are loud or soft and the concepts could be reinforced through movement

15. ROCK A BYE BABY

C15

Purpose

To give children practice in moving in time to the underlying beat of a song and in singing softly; to reinforce the notion of 'down', in preparation for future pitch-related activities; to introduce children to the process of composing by telling a story through sounds.

Resources

Glockenspiel and xylophone, each arranged so that there is a removable sticky label on the note E. Each instrument should be upended so that the smaller, narrower, higher-pitched end is raised on a set of books; cassette: side 1, track 9; Copymaster 15; understanding of the term 'glissando' (see glossary p. 108); space for movement.

Activity

Ask the children how many of them have baby sisters or brothers at home. How difficult is it to get the baby to sleep sometimes? What do they or their parents do to help? They will probably mention rocking movements. Do they or their parents ever sing to the baby? How important is it to be as quiet as possible when the baby is going off to sleep? Guide the discussion round to the way that lullabies include rocking movements and soft, gentle sounds.

It might be useful to show them pictures of old fashioned cradles to show them how the rockers were designed specifically to help lull the child to sleep. Describe how, in the lullaby you are going to sing, the baby's cradle has not got rockers. It has been put in the tree to help it sway backwards and forwards. But then look what happens when the wind rises!

Sing the song to the children, making rocking movements as you do so. Then teach it to the children and invite them to copy the movement.

ROCK A BYE BABY			
Starting note: E. Count in: 1-2 1-2			
Rock	a	bye	ba	by
1			2	
E			E	
on	the	tree	top_____.	
1			2	
E			E	
When	the	wind	blows the	
1			2	
E			E	

Cra	dle will	rock.	
1		2	
E		E	
When	the bough	breaks the	
1		2	
E		E	
Cra	dle will	fall.	
1		2	
E		E	
Down	will come	ba	by
1		2	
E		E	
Cra	dle and	all.	
1		2	
E		E	

When they have had some practice in this, focus on singing the song softly so that the baby does not wake up.

Play the note E several times, firstly on the glockenspiel and then on the xylophone. Which do they think produces the softer sound? (The xylophone, hopefully.) Now ask the children to sing the song with you while you accompany them on the xylophone. You could invite individual children to provide this accompaniment after a while.

Ask the children to spread out and stand in their own space within the room. Sing the song again. This time on the words 'down will come baby cradle and all', the children sink to the ground and you play a downward glissando to accompany this. Again, the accompaniment idea could be passed to an individual child.

Extension

Ask the children to find a space as before. This time play a downward glissando and an upward glissando. As you do so the children sink down and rise up accordingly. The notion of down and up could be further developed at other times in the school day. For example, when they are playing on large apparatus, you could play a downward glissando when children are going down the slide and notes going up in pitch as they climb up the ladder again.

Telling the story with sounds

Ask the children to look at the pictures of the events in the story on **Copymaster 15**. Discuss with them what is happening. In the first picture, the baby is rocking gently. How will the wind sound at that point? (Very soft.) Can anyone try to make a sound like the sound of soft wind with their voices? Try this individually and as a group.

What is happening in the second picture? (The clouds are gathering and the wind is building up.) What kind of sound can they make with their voices to show that the wind is building up? Try this individually and as a group. This time, the sounds will need to be considerably louder.

Then what happens? (The branch suddenly snaps.) What kind of sound could they make to give the impression of a breaking bough? At this point try out instrumental as well as vocal sounds. They could say words like 'Crack!' very loudly and try making a very loud noise on a wooden guiro. This might also be accompanied by a clashing cymbal sound. Then, as the cradle comes down, the children could play a downward glissando on the tuned percussion.

These are simply suggestions to help you. If you, or the children, have other alternatives which you prefer,

then by all means use them. When you have discussed and tried out the ideas, try to put them together into one sequence. You might need to give spoken instructions at first as to when to come in or stop. Try to help the children respond to visual cues as soon as possible. You might, for example, point to a group that is supposed to come in. Or you could point to the part of the picture which is being illustrated at that particular moment. After a while, individual children could take on the role of directing the performance. When you have practised the piece a few times, try recording it on tape and playing it back to them.

In both the performance and listening activities, emphasise the importance of listening to each other, watching, and not talking. It will take time for the children to master such an approach but do not delay introducing it. Also, when the children have listened to their own performance, ask them if there are any ways in which they think it could be made better. In this way you will be helping them to begin to look for other possibilities in what they are producing – an essential element in creating anything.

Rock a bye ba - by on the tree top. When the wind blows the

cra - dle will rock. When the bough breaks the

cra - dle will fall. Down will come ba - by, cra - dle and all.

16. LULLABY COMPOSITION

Make up a lullaby to rock a baby, or doll or teddy, to sleep. Start by asking the children to move in a rocking way. Then ask them to make up some words which will help the teddy go to sleep. Next, ask them to make up a tune. It will probably be very simple but, since the

children at this stage often make up their own tunes whilst playing alone or in groups, it should prove a rewarding and far easier exercise than it might at first seem.

25

17. SOFT AND LOUD SOUNDS ON ONE INSTRUMENT

C16

Purpose
To give children further practice in identifying sounds as loud or soft; to help children experiment with producing loud and soft sounds on instruments.

Resources
A large tambour or drum and grains of rice placed on its surface; Copymaster 16.

Activity
Play a series of sounds on the tambour. After each sound has been produced, ask the children to identify whether the sound was loud or soft. Help the children scatter the rice grains in the centre of the tambour. Then play a series of sounds as before and ask them to identify not only whether the sound is loud or soft but also what happens to the grains in each instance. (The louder the sound, the more the grains will jump.)

Now ask the children to play the tambour softly or loudly, using the amount of grain jumping as a way of helping them refine their aural perceptions of the loudness or softness of the sounds played.

Extension
Present the children with the **Copymaster 16**. Discuss with them which of the drums are being played loudly and which are being played softly. How can they tell which drums are which? (In the case of the loud drums, the grains are leaping higher.)

18. LOUD AND SOFT SOUNDS AROUND US

C14, 17

Purpose
To help the children extend their awareness of loud and soft sounds – particularly in relation to environmental sounds.

Resources
Copymasters 14 and 17.

Activity
Tell the children that, in a moment, you are going to ask them to sit extremely quietly and listen to the sounds around them. Ask them to try to remember what they have heard in that space of time.

When they have sat in silence for a short time, help them to make a list of the sounds which they have heard. Write the word for each sound, together with a drawing, on a separate card if necessary. Now discuss with them whether they thought the sounds were loud or soft and arrange the cards accordingly into two piles. You could also ask them to label the sounds using the appropriate word from **Copymaster 14.**

Look at **Copymaster 17**. Discuss with the children what is being illustrated in each case. Which object or activity will make a loud noise and which will make a soft sound. Ask the children to colour the soft ones in one colour and the loud ones in another colour. Alternatively, you could make several photocopies of Copymaster 17, mount them on to card and cut out each picture. The children could sort them into 'loud' and 'soft' piles and label them accordingly.

Extension
This activity can be extended into a card game. The children sit in a circle, each with an equal number of randomly selected cards. The first sound snippet from the tape is played. If the first child has a card which corresponds to that sound, he or she puts it in the centre of the table. The second child is then asked to see whether they have the appropriate card for the second sound snippet and so on. The first child to put down all of their cards becomes the winner of the game.

You could also play two types of 'Snap' with such cards. In the first version, the children call 'snap' every time two identical pictures are put down. In the second, they call 'snap' if pictures of two objects which produce the same volume of sound are put down.

You could further extend this activity by letting the children listen to music of varying volumes. Pieces which are mainly soft include: 'Ase's death' from Peer Gynt Suite No.1 by Grieg, Debussy's *Clair de lune*. Loud pieces include: Janacek's *Sinfonietta*, opening of Bach's 'Toccata and fugue in D minor' for organ.

19. PETER HAMMERS WITH ONE HAMMER C18

Purpose
To give children practice in responding to the underlying pulse, or beat, of a song through a combination of movements of increasing complexity.

Resources
Copymaster 18; cassette: side 1, track 10.

Activity
Teach the children the song 'Peter hammers with one hammer'.

PETER HAMMERS WITH ONE HAMMER			
Starting note: D. Count in: 1-2 1-2			
Peter	hammers with	one	hammer,
1	2	1	2
One	hammer,	one	hammer.
1	2	1	2
Peter	hammers with	one	hammer,
1	2	1	2
Then he	hammers with	two_____	.
1	2	1	2

Peter hammers with two hammers, two hammers, two hammers,

Peter hammers with two hammers, then he hammers with three, etc.

On verse 1, they mark the beat with one fist movement; on verse two with two fist movements; on verse three with two fists and one foot; on verse four with two fists and two feet; on verse five with two fists, two feet and a head nod.

Extension
For this you will need **Copymaster 18.** Mount the sheet on card and cut out the various sections. Perform the song again. This time, however, rearrange the sequence of activities so that they do not simply progress in order from one to five. Later, the children themselves could take turns in deciding on the order in which the movements are to be produced. A further variation involves dividing the class in half, with one half following one sequence of movements and the other half a different sequence. Some young children might, however, find this too difficult.

There are many traditional counting songs. You might wish to teach the children some of these and integrate them into your other work in the curriculum; particularly in the area of maths.

Pe - ter ha - mmers with one ha - mmer, one ha - mmer, one ha - mmer.

Pe - ter ha - mmers with one ha - mmer, then he ha - mmers with two.

20. WE'LL CLAP HANDS TOGETHER

C19

Purpose
To give children practice in moving in time to the steady beat or pulse of a song, using a variety of movements.

Resources
Copymaster 19; chime bars F and C; cassette: side 1, track 11.

Activity
Sit the children in a circle on chairs and teach them the first verse of the song:

WE'LL CLAP HANDS TOGETHER			
Starting note: F. Count in: 1-2-3-4			
We'll clap hands to	ge		ther.
1	2	3	4
We'll clap hands to	ge		ther.
1	2	3	4
We'll clap hands to	ge		ther and
1	2	3	4
Have a wonderful time____.			
1	2	3	4

When they can perform the words adequately, add the clap on each beat, and ask the children to copy you.

Move on from there to teach the words and gestures for the other verses:

We'll shake hands to	ge		ther, etc.
1	2	3	4
We'll tap	knees to	ge	ther, etc.
1	2	3	4
We'll stamp feet to		ge	ther, etc.
1	2	3	4

Introduce each new movement by referring to **Copymaster 19**.

Extension
Invite individual children to rearrange the pictures to produce new sequences of actions.

Invite the children to think up new gestures and new text to describe them which can be fitted into the song.

Play the chime bars F and C (as shown) to accompany the children's singing.

Count in: 1-2 3-4			
	F-C F-C		
We'll clap hands to	ge		ther
F	C	F	C
We'll clap hands to	ge		ther
F	C	F	C
We'll clap hands to	ge		ther and
F	C	F	C
Have a wonderful time_____.			
F	C	F	C

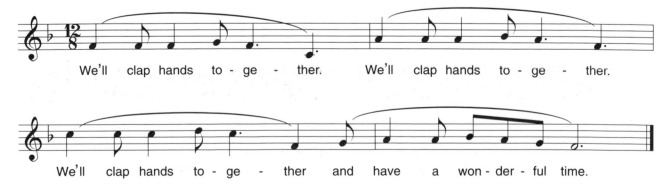

28

21. WHAT SOUNDS CAN WE MAKE WITH OUR BODIES?

Purpose
To give children practice in exploring body sounds.

Activity
Play the following copying game:

Sit the children in a circle so that they can all see you easily. Tell them that you are going to make a gesture, such as clapping your hands, and they must copy you. Then, as you say 'Change' you will start a new action which they must then copy.

When the children have had some practice at this, refine the activity so that they not only have to produce the action but also have to make the sound loud or soft, or fast or slow just in the way that you are making it. After a while, let the children take turns at leading the activity.

This game is a very useful one and can be adapted and extended in various ways to suit several stages of pupil development. One variation would be to play the game as before, changing your movement, however, a little

while before instructing the children to change. This means that the children will have to produce one action, observe another action and prepare to reproduce the action being observed. This type of sequence is a considerable aid to concentration and is a useful pre-notation reading skill.

Another variation is to arrange the children so that they are sitting in a circle. One child sits blindfolded in the centre. A second child sits behind the first and makes a noise with their hands. The blindfolded child must then try to copy the sound using the same means of sound generation.

Both of the games described in this section can be extended to include more complex sounds. The second game could also be extended to involve sequences of sounds (e.g clap, snap, rub) and sounds involving other parts of the body. Until you and the children have built up sufficient confidence, do not be afraid to keep things simple.

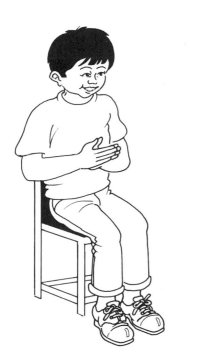
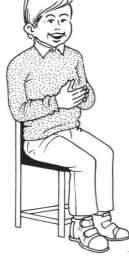

22. WHAT CAN WE DO WITH OUR HANDS?

C20, 48

Purpose
To give children practice in marking the underlying beat or pulse of a song with a variety of gestures; to extend the exploration of body sounds; to give children practice in performing sounds indicated by a preliminary form of notation; to give children experience of directing and being directed in the performance of a short improvisation based on body sounds.

Resources
Copymasters 20 and 48; cassette: side 1, track 12.

Activity
Arrange the children in a circle sitting on chairs and teach them the following song:

WHAT CAN WE DO WITH OUR HANDS?							
Starting note: F. Count in: 1-2-3-4 1-2-3-4							
What	can	we	do	with our hands?	clap	clap	clap
1	2	3	4	1	2	3	4
What	can	we	do	with our feet?	stamp	stamp	stamp
1	2	3	4	1	2	3	4
What	can	we	do	with our hands and		feet	as
1	2	3	4	1	2	3	4
We	walk	down the		street?	clap	clap	clap
					stamp	stamp	stamp
1	2	3	4	1	2	3	4

Perform the song loudly the first time, then softly. Accompany the words 'clap' and 'stamp' with the appropriate gestures.

Read the following poem:

HANDS
 Hands are very handy things,
 Hands can wash things,
 Hands can squash things,
 Hands can gently pat your head.

Hands can clap,
Hands can flap,
Hands can point like this or that.
Hands can make things,
Hands can shake things,
Hands can flutter just like wings.
Hands can fold,
Hands can hold,
Hands are very handy things.
 By Ogden Nash, from *Wordplay*, Puffin.

Accompany the reading and subsequent reciting of the above poem with movements. (These could be projected on to a screen to produce a shadow play.) Focus on the line which refers to the way that hands can clap. Then move the discussion to a consideration of what other sounds can be produced with hands.

Now play the Change Game described in activity 21, focussing particularly on hand sounds. Make a chart of the sounds, e.g. pictures of hands clapping with accompanying labels. Also discuss whether the sounds produced are loud or soft.

Extension
Make several copies of **Copymasters 20** and **48**, mount them on to card and cut them into separate pictures. Arrange them in a variety of sequences and ask individual children to conduct the rest of the class in performing the types of sounds shown. When they have practised this, extend the activity so that the sound gestures on two cards are performed simultaneously. The children can try out and discuss which effects they like.

Play the children a recording of gospel singers. Draw their attention to the way that these singers make use of clapping hands and how often it is an integral element in their performances.

What can we do with our hands? *clap, clap, clap.* What can we do with our
feet? *stamp, stamp, stamp.* What can we do with our hands and feet as
we walk down the street? *clap, clap, clap. stamp, stamp, stamp.*

23. SEE-SAW DOWN ON THE FLOOR

Purpose

To help children develop the spatial concept of down and up in preparation for later pitch work; to give children further practice in moving in time to the beat or pulse of a rhyme.

Resources

Tambour and beater; chime bars C and G; cassette: side 1, track 13.

Activity

Teach the children the following song:

SEE-SAW DOWN ON THE FLOOR

Starting note: G.   Count in: 1-2 1-2

See -	saw	down on	the floor.
1	2	1	2
G	C	G	C

Up again	onto	your	feet_____.
1	2	1	2
G	C	G	C

Little girl	lost her	white	cap
1	2	1	2
G	C	G	C

Walking	down the	street_____.	
1	2	1	2
G	C	G	C

When they can sing the song fairly confidently ask them to tap out the beat gently on their laps as they sing

it. Later, individual children could transfer the hand tap into a beat on the tambour.

Next, arrange the children in a circle facing you. As they sing the words 'down on the floor' ask them to copy you as you crouch down. Then, on the words 'up again on to your feet', ask them to straighten up again. When they are able to do this without your help, add the chime bar accompaniment as indicated. Draw the children's attention to the way the music goes down in pitch with them as they go down and how it rises up again as they straighten up.

'Up again onto your feet'

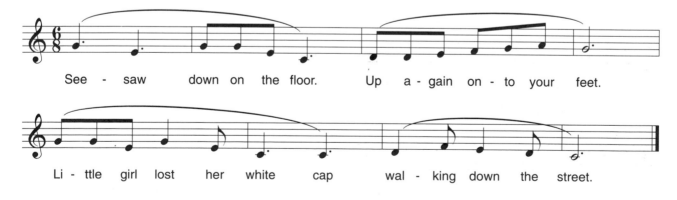

24. COMPOSING WITH BODY SOUNDS

C21

Purpose

To introduce children to composing their own piece of music, using body sounds.

Resources

Copymaster 21; recording of storm music, e.g. storm section from Britten's 'Noyes Fludde'.

Activity

Repeat the Change Game from activity 21. Focus particularly on producing a wide range of hand, feet and vocal sounds. Now look at the pictures on **Copymaster 21** and discuss them with the children.

Next look at each picture separately and discuss what kinds of sounds we might hear in each case. In picture one there is likely to be a very soft gentle breeze. How could they make sounds to represent this? (They could make a very quiet hissing sound with their mouths or they could rub the palms of their hands together very gently.) In picture two, the rain is beginning to fall. How could they represent this? (They could tap the backs of their hands or their laps with their fingers – at first very slowly and then gradually more quickly.) In picture three, they might represent the extremely heavy rainfall by drumming their fingers even more quickly on the floor or a table top. Encourage them to experiment with the effects produced when several people do this and when the whole class does it. How could they represent the thunder claps in picture four? (They might clap their hands together very loudly or stamp both feet on the ground. Again the different effects produced when different numbers of children perform a sound could be explored).

Now discuss with them what happens as the storm abates and eventually the sun comes out again. They might decide simply to play all the sound sections in reverse or they might wish to vary the effects. When all the individual sections have been tried out and practised, put the whole piece together and record the result. (It must be emphasised that the ideas for producing sounds outlined above are no more than suggestions to prompt your own thinking and to help that of the children. If the children have different ideas then they must be encouraged to try them out, discuss them and accept modify or reject them.)

Vary the above approach by having different groups working with you at different times on one picture each, before the whole composition is put together. Whenever the children have completed a composition, it is important that they should have the opportunity to perform it and also to listen to and comment on the effects which they have produced. They should also have the opportunity to listen to related works by other composers so that they can see that they are not working in isolation. In this case, it would be very useful to listen to a composition depicting a storm or a piece which also makes use of body sounds.

Extension

Play Britten's 'Noyes Fludde' to the children and draw their attention to the way the music starts with the low pitched instruments depicting the movements of the waves. Then the raindrops are represented by the sounds made by hitting drinking mugs of different pitches slung on a string. Later the recorders represent the sound of the wind. They will also hear the lightning being represented by sharp, cracking sounds. Then at the height of the storm, Noah, his family and all the animals can be heard singing a prayer for safe deliverance.

Resist the temptation to tell the children beforehand what they will hear. Instead, let them hear the music first and then help them to identify the above features through discussion and further listening. Further examples of storm music and music about the weather which you might find useful are: Debussy, 'Jardins sous la Pluie' from *Estampes*; Arnold, Overture 'Tam O'Shanter'; Britten, 'Sea Interludes' from *Peter Grimes*; Chopin, 'Raindrop' Prelude.

After listening to the recordings of other composers' music, the children could be encouraged to think of changes which they could make to their own composition. In this case, for example, they might decide to change the order of the various sections. This could easily be done by rearranging the original pictures. Such reworking of an idea at however elementary a level will help the children begin to see that there are many possibilities inherent in any composition.

You might at this, or a later stage, wish to repeat this exercise involving instruments. Do not be too anxious to involve too many different types of sound sources at one time because the children could end up spending more time on deciding which instrument to use rather than on finding what can be done with that one particular instrument.

25. SEE-SAW MARGERY DAW

C22, 23

Purpose

To give children practice in moving in time to the pulse or beat of a song; to help develop the concept of up and down movement in preparation for later work on pitch development; to enable the child to convert upward and downward physical movements into upward and downward melodic movements and vice versa.

Resources

Voices; see-saw (if possible); wooden agogo; glockenspiel or xylophone; Copymasters 22 and 23; cassette: side 1, track 14; wooden agogo chime bars E and C.

Activity

Teach the children the song 'See-saw Margery Daw'. Arrange for pairs of children to take turns on the see-saw. The whole class, including the children on the see-saw, sing the song as the see-saw moves up and down in time to the beat of the music. (If there is no see-saw available, the children can work in pairs on imaginary see-saws.) Hold the wooden agogo in your left hand with the smaller cylinder to the right. Hold the beater in the right hand and tap out the beat on the relevant syllables (as indicated below), alternating between the right and left cylinders as you do so.

SEE-SAW MARGERY DAW

Starting note: E   Count in: 1-2 1-2

See	-	saw
1		2
Margery		Daw.
1		2
Johnny shall		have a new
1		2
ma		ster.
1		2
He shall		have but a
1		2
penny a		day if
1		2
he cannot		work any
1		2
fa		ster.
1		2

When they have gained confidence in this activity, ask the children to find themselves a space each, at various points around the room. This time, the children work separately, moving up and down as they sing the song. As they do so, accompany their movements with an upward and downward glissando (see glossary) on the tuned instrument to match the movement. Arrange the glockenspiel or xylophone so that the higher-pitched end is raised up on a number of books. Thus, the upward and downward movements in pitch will be matched by the physical movements upward and downward of the beater. At a later point, the children themselves could take responsibility for providing the glissando accompaniment. You might also find some children who could manage the agogo accompaniment.

Introduce the children to the pictures of a see-saw on **Copymaster 22.** Draw their attention to the upward and downward movements. Make several photocopies of these, mount them on to card and mix them up. Then ask the children to select all the ones which are going up and all the ones which are going down, etc.

Arrange for two children to play the game on a real, or imaginary, see-saw. Arrange two tuned percussion instruments, each up-ended, on the right and left of the see-saw. As the child on the right comes down, the instrumentalist on that side echoes the movement with a downward glissando. At the same time, the instrumentalist on the left hand side plays an upward moving glissando to reflect the movement of the child on that end of the see-saw.

Another similar activity involves asking the children to find a space in the room with their backs to you. Explain to them that you are going to play an upward or downward glissando on the tuned instrument. (At this stage a word like a 'slide' – a slide up or a slide down – will be a better term to help the children understand what is meant.) They must listen carefully and move up or down accordingly. This will enable them to convert sounds into signs.

A further activity, which will also prepare them for later work in reading and writing music, involves their converting signs into sounds. The children work in pairs. One child chooses to make a movement upwards or downwards and the second child then matches that movement with an appropriate movement upwards or downwards on the tuned instrument.

Make several copies of **Copymaster 23.** Mount them on cards and cut them into smaller cards with one arrow on each. Use these as the basis for discussing and identifying up and down movements. The children could then be asked to group them into sets: all the

upward movements together, all the downward movements together, opposite movements together, etc. These could also become the basis for simple card games.

For example, each child could be given an equal number of random cards. The first child puts down a card. The next one must put down a card showing an opposite movement, etc. If a child cannot put a card down, they can take a card from a pile. The first child to get rid of all their cards wins the game.

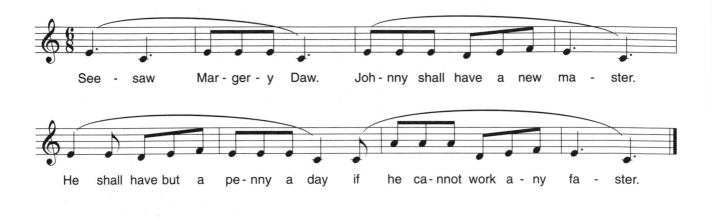

See - saw Mar - ger - y Daw. Joh - nny shall have a new ma - ster.

He shall have but a pe - nny a day if he ca - nnot work a - ny fa - ster.

26. HUMPTY DUMPTY

C24–26

Purpose
To give children practice in responding to the beat of a song through movement; to give them the opportunity to encounter, test out and learn the names of new instruments; to help reinforce the concept of downward movement in music; to enable children to select instruments which they think would help accompany and illustrate a song.

Resources
Cassette: side 1, track 15; xylophone with all bars on it and upended so that the small, high pitched bars are at the top (see diagram); a beater with a face drawn on it to represent Humpty; tambour; claves and a range of other unpitched percussion instruments; Copymasters 24–6.

Activity
Say the rhyme to the children and ask them to recite it back to you. (Many of them will no doubt know it already.) Then teach them the tune.

HUMPTY DUMPTY			
Starting note: E. Count in: 1-2 1-2			
Hump - ty	Dump - ty	sat on a	wall.
1	2	1	2
Hump - ty	Dump - ty	had a great	fall.
1	2	1	2

All the king's horses and all the king's			men
1	2	1	2
Couldn't put	Humpty to- ge- ther	a	gain.
1	2	1	2

When they can sing the tune fairly fluently, ask the children to tap out the beat on the appropriate syllables as indicated above. They can do this by tapping their laps or clapping, or through a combination of movements. Instead of sitting down, the class could walk around in a circle holding hands. On the words 'had a great fall', all the children fall down. Alternatively, the children could pretend to be on horseback as the king's men and trot round the circle in time to the beat or they could make arm movements as they sit in their places. There is no reason why a combination of movements should not be used to suit the differing capabilities of the children in your class. Those children who can already move accurately in time to the beat could be invited to accompany the song on an untuned percussion instrument as the others step or tap the beat.

Extension
Look at the pictures of the successive events in the nursery rhyme on **Copymaster 24–6** and discuss with the children how these might be represented. How

34

could they show Humpty falling? (They could have a downward glissando on the xylophone followed by a crash.) Which instrument would be best for the crash? (Possibly the drum or the cymbal, or a combination of these.) How could we show the king's horses coming? (Possibly by means of the wooden agogo or claves.) Help the children to explore the various sounds that the available instruments produce and to select an appropriate sound. Make sure that you use the opportunity to give a name to the instruments as they are introduced. (Pictures of the instruments could be labelled and made into a classroom display.) When they have decided which instruments are to be used for each

section, let the children make drawings of them in the spaces provided on the copymasters. Then put the sections together and let them perform from their 'score'.

You could involve one group in producing the musical illustrations to all three sections. Alternatively, you could ask separate groups to work on individual sections. You might also have more than one group working on the composition so that you end up with more than one piece. As an extension to this last arrangement, you could ask one group to perform another group's score. This would make the activity of preparing a score more purposeful.

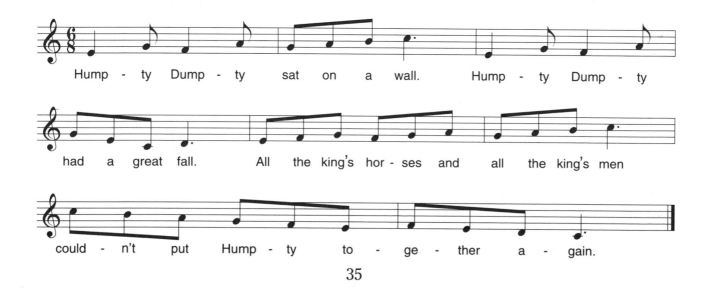

Hump - ty Dump - ty sat on a wall. Hump - ty Dump - ty

had a great fall. All the king's hor - ses and all the king's men

could - n't put Hump - ty to - ge - ther a - gain.

27. MARCH MARCH

Purpose

To give children practice in moving in time to the beat or pulse of a rhyme; to help children develop the ability to produce and identify accented beats; to emphasise the notion that beats can move at different speeds from one performance of a piece to another.

Resources

Cassette: side 1, track 16; metronome; a space suitable for movement.

Activity

So far, the children have been fairly sedentary when marking the beat. Now give them more practice in moving around. Let them move around in a circle, chanting or singing the following rhyme while marking the beat with their feet. To help them differentiate between the feet, tie a ribbon round their left legs and show how that is the one to start. Lift it ready to come down on the first beat. Although this rhyme is very simple, the accompanying movements might take quite a time for some children to master.

Accenting the beat while marching

MARCH MARCH			
Starting note: D.	Count in:	Left right	left right
		1 - 2	1 - 2
March,	march,	marching	by.
Left	right	left	right
Left,	right,	head up	high.
Left	right	left	right
On,	on,	on we	go.
Left	right	left	right
Right up	to the	ca	stle.
Left	right	left	right

When the children have gained some confidence in performing this activity, accent the left beat by saying or singing it more loudly and by asking the children to clap as well as stepping on that beat.

Extension

Make a series of footprints out of card. You could draw round the children's own feet when doing this. Arrange the card feet on the floor to indicate a pathway which a child must follow. Experiment with moving the footprints closer together and further apart and asking the children to step on them at a regular pace. What do they notice? (The closer the footprints are to each other, the quicker the pace; the further apart, the slower the pace.) Chant the rhyme several times indicating different speeds for the initial count and therefore for the beat in successive performances. Set the metronome at varying paces and perform the rhyme in time with the various settings.

Play other marches to your class. Most record shops will have a considerable selection of marches, particularly military marches. Some suggestions are: Bizet, March from *'Jeux d'Enfants'*; Coates, 'Dambusters' March'; Goldman, 'Children's March'; Strauss, 'The Radetsky March'; Tchaikovsky, 'March of the Tin Soldiers' from 'Album for the Young'; Walton, 'Crown Imperial'. Play short extracts and do so several times to increase the children's familiarity with the music. March music creates numerous possibilities for movement in time to the music.

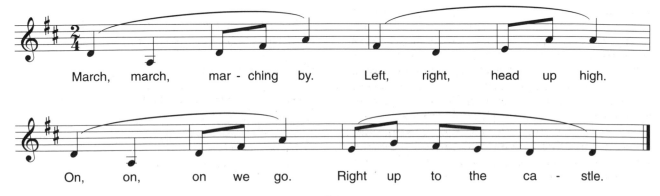

March, march, mar - ching by. Left, right, head up high.

On, on, on we go. Right up to the ca - stle.

28. THE MAGIC INSTRUMENTS

Purpose
To help children identify and react through movement to the varying timbres of pairs of instruments.

Resources
Two instruments which differ considerably from each other in the type of sound which they produce (e.g. a metal and a skin instrument such as a glockenspiel and a drum); a space suitable for movement.

Activity
Make up a story to tell the children about two magic instruments e.g. a glockenspeil and a drum. One of them (e.g. the drum) makes people move, the other (the glockenspiel) prevents them from moving. Describe an adventure where someone escapes from danger because the drum made them move. In another instance, someone is saved from falling off a cliff because the glockenspiel sounds in time, freezing the person to the spot.

Now play a version of 'Simon Says' with the children. Explain that if you ask them to do something (such as stretching or touching their toes) when the drum is playing, they must perform that activity. But if you ask them to do something when the glockenspiel is playing, they must not move. Anyone who moves in response to the wrong instrument is out. The winner is the last child out. This game can be varied by allowing the children themselves to take turns as leaders. The instrument pairs should also be varied so that the children's experience of, and ability to identify, instruments is extended.

Moving when the drum sounds

29. GOOSEY GOOSEY GANDER

Purpose
To give children practice in responding to the underlying regular beat of a song with a combination of movements; to help reinforce the concept of 'up' and 'down' in relation to music, in preparation for later work on pitch development; to give children practice in converting sounds into signs and signs into sounds in relation to basic pitch work.

Resources
You will need the smallest (i.e. highest pitched) and largest (i.e. lowest pitched) chime bars from the set. Arrange the highest pitched note on a high level, such as a table, and the lowest pitched one on the floor. You will also need an up-ended glockenspiel or xylophone as shown in the diagram overleaf. The instrument should be arranged so that the high sounding part is propped up on books. In this way the physical movement up and down will illustrate the melodic upwards and downwards movement. You will also need the cassette: side 1, track 17; voices; space for movement; Copymasters 27–8.

Activity
Teach the children the song:

GOOSEY GOOSEY GANDER			
Starting note: C. Count in: 1-2-3-4 1-2-3-4			
Goosey	goosey	gan	der,
1	2	3	4
*	*	*	*
Whither	do you	wan	der?
1	2	3	4
*	*	*	*
Up	stairs and	down	stairs and
1	2	3	4
↑	↑	↓	↓
HC	HC	LC	LC

In my	lady's	cham	ber
1	2	3	4
*	*	*	*

There I	met an	old	man who
1	2	3	4
*	*	*	*

Wouldn't	say his	prayers.	I
1	2	3	4
*	*	*	*

Took him	by the	left	leg and
1	2	3	4
*	*	*	*

Threw him	down the	stairs____.	
1	2	3	4
↓	↓	↓	↓
LC	LC	LC	LC

* = Knee pat	HC = High chime bar
↑ = Point up	LC = Low chime bar
↓ = Point down	

Visualising high and low notes

The children sing the song. On the words 'upstairs and downstairs', they move their hands up and down accordingly. As they do so, the teacher plays the high chime bar and the low chime bar as indicated.

Extension
As a variation on this, the upward and downward movements could be accompanied by upward and downward glissando slides on the glockenspiel or xylophone. Later, the children themselves could take turns in providing the background instrumental work.

Make several copies of the pictures of the upended glockenspiel on **Copymaster 27** and also of the 'up' or 'down' labels on **Copymaster 28.** Arrange the children in pairs with their backs to each other. One child plays a glissando going in one direction (up or down) on the glockenspiel or xylophone. The second child then has to put the appropriate arrow pointing in the right direction on Copymaster 27.

This activity can be varied in several ways. For example, the child on the xylophone could play several glissandi: up-down; up-down-up; up-up-down-down, etc. which the second child then has to record. Another version would be for one child to place several arrows pointing up or down which a second child then has to convert into appropriate sounds.

Goo - sey goo - sey gan - der, whi - ther do you wan - der?

Up stairs and down stairs and in my la - dy's cham - ber.

There I met an old man who would - n't say his prayers. I

took him by the left leg and threw him down the stairs.

38

30. MUSIC ABOUT BIRDS

Play the children selections from Mussorgsky's 'Ballet of the Unhatched Chickens' from 'Pictures at an Exhibition' and Saint-Saëns' 'The Swan' from 'Carnival of the Animals'. Draw their attention to the way that, in the first of these pieces, Mussorgsky creates an impression of the chickens' clucking and pecking by using high sounding instruments and by emphasising some notes unexpectedly and irregularly. When the class has listened to the piece a few times, encourage them to make pecking movements and to move in the irregular way suggested by the music.

Show them how very different the Saint-Saëns piece is. Here the music is flowing and gentle like the movements of a swan. Give the children the opportunity to try to produce similar gentle, flowing movements. They could do this with the music or after they have heard it. You could also draw their attention to the way

that the music is now played on a cello as opposed to the high pitched instruments heard in the Mussorgsky piece.

Listening to pitch
Describe to the children the type of birds which fly particularly high up into the air. Play the opening of 'The Lark Ascending' by Vaughan Williams. Draw their attention to the way that the violin melody rises higher and higher in pitch just as the lark rises up. You could reinforce this notion by asking the children to spread around the room and, starting from a crouching position, stretch themselves as high as possible as the tune gets higher. (As an example of high pitched instruments, in this case the piccolo and flute, you could play the 'Chinese Dance' from 'The Nutcracker Suite' by Tchaikovsky.)

31. IDENTIFYING INSTRUMENTS

C29–33

Purpose
To give children further practice in exploring the capabilities of a range of instruments and in identifying their tone colours.

Resources
A small number of instruments, e.g. drum, triangle, castanets, tambourine; cassette: side 1, track 18; Copymasters 29–33; chime bars G and D.

Activity
Teach the children the song 'Listen to the sound of the great big drum'.

LISTEN TO THE SOUND OF THE GREAT BIG DRUM

Starting note: G.   Count in 1-2-3-4 1-2-3-4

Listen to the sound of the great big drum — boom!

1	2	3	4	1	2	3	4
D	G	D	G	D	G D		G

Listen to the sound of the great big drum — boom!

1	2	3	4	1	2	3	4
D	G	D	G	D	G D		G

Listen to the sound of the great big drum — boom!

1	2	3	4	1	2	3	4
D	G	D	G	D	G D		G

Boom!   Boom!   Boom!

1	2	3	4	1	2	3	4
D	G	D	G	D	G D		G

Listen to the sound of the castanet — click (x3)
Click.   Click.   Click.

Listen to the sound of the tambourine — shake (x3)
Shake.   Shake.   Shake.

Listen to the sound of the triangle — ting (x3)
Ting.   Ting.   Ting.

39

Start by singing the song through. Then add the instruments on the words 'boom', 'shake', 'ting', etc. When the children are familiar with the song, encourage them to add the names of other instruments with words to describe the sounds which they produce.

Play the 'Identifying game'. Sit the children in two rows with their backs to each other. In front of each row place an identical set of the instruments which the children have already encountered and with whose sounds they have already become familiar. At a signal from you, the first child in row A gets up and plays one of the instruments. That child's counterpart in row B is now required to play the same instrument. The game continues in this way until the row with the higher number of correct answers wins the game.

You can vary this game in several ways: by increasing the number of instruments involved; by involving two instruments simultaneously; by asking children to reproduce the precise order in which a series of instruments is played; by asking the children to reproduce specific rhythmic patterns as well as the sequence of instruments.

Extension
Make several photocopies of the instruments on **Copymasters 29–33** and of the labels and involve the children in matching pictures to their sounds. You will notice that some blank cards have also been included. These allow the children themselves to find words to describe the sounds made by the instruments. You could then help them to write those onto the blank cards.

Make this activity into a card game. Each child is given a random set of equal numbered cards. If a child has a matching picture and sound (e.g. triangle and 'ting') that pair is put in the centre of the table. When all players have put existing pairs down, one player takes a card from the person on the right and tries to match it with one already in hand. The game then continues in a clockwise direction, with each player taking a card from the player on the right. Whenever a pair of cards is formed, it is put on the table. The child who gets rid of their cards first is the winner.

Needless to say, all these activities cannot be pursued in one go at this point. You will need to intersperse them amongst later activities and ensure that they are varied to suit the range of different capabilities amongst the children in the class at any one time.

Listen to recordings of several of the instruments on which the children have been experimenting. For the sound of the castanets, listen to *'España'* by Chabrier. Listen to 'Fossils' from Saint-Saëns 'Carnival of the Animals' for the sound of the xylophone. The glockenspiel can be heard in 'Little Bells' from Elgar's 'Wand of Youth Suite No. 2'.

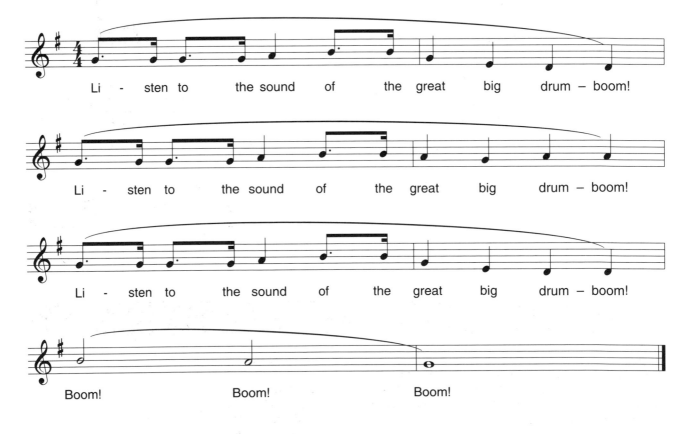

Li - sten to the sound of the great big drum – boom!

Li - sten to the sound of the great big drum – boom!

Li - sten to the sound of the great big drum – boom!

Boom!   Boom!   Boom!

32. WHO WILL COME INTO OUR LITTLE RING?

Purpose
To give children further practice in moving in time to the underlying beat or pulse of a song.

Resources
Cassette: side 1, track 19; chime bars D and A; space for movement.

Activity
Teach them the following song.

WHO WILL COME INTO OUR LITTLE RING?

Starting note: A.   Count in: 1-2-3-4 1-2-3-4

Who	will	come	into	our	little	ring	and
1	2	3	4	1	2	3	4
A	D	A	D	A	D	A	D

Make it a	little	bit	bi			gger?	
1	2	3	4	1	2	3	4
A	D	A	D	A	D	A	D

Who	will	come	into	our	little	ring	and
1	2	3	4	1	2	3	4
A	D	A	D	A	D	A	D

Make it a	little	bit	bi			gger?	
1	2	3	4	1	2	3	4
A	D	A	D	A	D	A	D

John will come into our little ring, etc.

Who will come into our little ring, etc.

Teach the children the words and music of the song. Then let them link hands and walk round in a circle stepping in time to the beat and singing the first verse. At the end of that verse the child who is standing at the front of a nearby line steps into the circle. The children now continue to sing the second verse but this time mentioning the new child's name, e.g. 'John will come into our little ring '. The first verse 'who will come' is then repeated and, on the third rendition, the next child joins, etc. This game could be played with more than one ring moving at a time. When the children have grasped the tune and the movements, add the two note accompaniment on the chime bars.

Who will come in - to our li - ttle ring, and make it a li - ttle bit bi - gger?

Who will come in - to our li - ttle ring and make it a li - ttle bit bi - gger?

33. FIVE LITTLE DUCKS

C34

Purpose
To give children further practice in moving in time to the pulse or beat of a song; to give them practice in simple accompaniment; to give them practice in starting and stopping to play on cue.

Resources
Cassette: side 1, track 20; space large enough for movement; two chime bars, A and D; a selection of five unpitched percussion instruments; Copymaster 34.

Activity
Read the following poem to the children:

A PIG TALE

Poor Jane Higgins
She had five piggins,
And one got drowned in the Irish Sea.
Poor Jane Higgins
She had four piggins,
And one flew over a sycamore tree.
Poor Jane Higgins
She had three piggins,
And one was taken away for pork.
Poor Jane Higgins
She had two piggins,

41

And one was sent to the Bishop of Cork.
Poor Jane Higgins
She had one piggin,
And that was struck by a shower of hail,
So poor Jane Higgins
She had no piggins,
And that's the end of the little pig tale.

© James Reeves from *The Wandering Moon and Other Poems* (Puffin Books) by James Reeves. Reprinted by permission of the James Reeves Estate.

Teach the children the following song:

FIVE LITTLE DUCKS

Starting note: D.   Count in: 1-2-3-4 1-2-3-4

Five	little	ducks	went	out	one	day,	
1	2	3	4	1	2	3	4
D	A	D	A	D	A	D	A

O	ver	the	hills	and	far	a	way.
1	2	3	4	1	2	3	4
D	A	D	A	D	A	D	A

One	little	duck	went	'quack,	quack,	quack',	
1	2	3	4	1	2	3	4
D	A	D	A	D	A	D	A

Four	little	ducks	came	waddling		back.	
1	2	3	4	1	2	3	4
D	A	D	A	D	A	D	A

Verse 2

Four little ducks, etc.

Verse 3

Three little ducks came waddling back.

Verse 4

Three little ducks, etc.

Verse 5

Two little ducks came waddling back.

Verse 6

Two little ducks, etc.

Verse 7

One little duck came waddling back.

Verse 8

One little duck, etc.

No little ducks came waddling back.

Verse 9

Mother duck went out one day,

Over the hills and far away.

Mother duck went 'quack, quack, quack,'

Five little ducks came waddling back.

As the children sing the song five of them walk around in single file moving their arms (wings) and feet in time to the music. One by one they drop out on cue. Then they all return again on the last line.

When they have grasped this, vary the activity by including a second group of five instrumentalists who play an accompaniment on the beat with a variety of untuned percussion instruments. Each player drops out on cue and then all return at the end.

42

Extension

The activity could be extended by adding the two note accompaniment on chime bars. This part could initially be played by you but later, if there are children who can manage it, they could take over the part.

Make several photocopies of **Copymaster 34**, mount them on to card and divide into individual pictures. When the children are adept at performing the song as described above, they could take turns at arranging the cards in different orders so that the number of performers changes.

As a follow up to this activity, play the children sections of 'The Duck' from 'Peter and the Wolf'. Draw their attention to the quacking sound produced by the oboe. Show them a picture of the oboe or try to arrange for them to see a real example of the instrument.

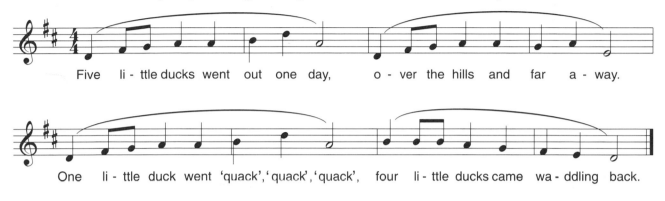

Five li - ttle ducks went out one day, o - ver the hills and far a - way.

One li - ttle duck went 'quack','quack','quack', four li - ttle ducks came wa - ddling back.

34. ROW, ROW, ROW THE BOAT

Purpose

To give children practice in moving in time to the steady beat of a song; to give children practice in marking the accented beats in a song via more exaggerated movements and through the use of instruments.

Resources

A poem or story about boats (find an appropriate one which talks about the gentle calmness of being in a rowing boat); a number of pictures of different types of boats – particularly rowing boats; cassette side 1, track 21; chime bars A and D.

Activity

Talk to the children about boats and the different types of boats that there are. Focus particularly on rowing boats and the way that, when they are well rowed, they glide smoothly along a river. You might wish to draw on a poem or on a simplified description of the characters from *Wind In The Willows* in their boat as another way into this activity. Teach the children the following song. Make sure that, when you are demonstrating, you are singing as smoothly and as gently as you can.

Merrily,	merrily,	merrily,	merrily.
In	out	in	out
D	A	D	A
Life is	just a	dream_____.	
In	out	in	out
D	A	D	A

When they have learnt the words and the tune to an adequate level, add the movements. To do this, the children sit on the floor and pretend to be in a rowing boat. They row in on the first and out on the second beat each time. Draw attention to the fact that they are supposed to be rowing gently. Use this to ensure that they do not sing too loudly and that their movements are smooth and gentle.

ROW, ROW, ROW THE BOAT			
Starting note: D. Count in: 1 - 2 1 - 2			
	In	out in	out
Row,	row,	row the	boat
In	out	in	out
D	A	D	A
Gently	down the	stream_____.	
In	out	in	out
D	A	D	A

Rowing singly

43

When they have done this, introduce the accompaniment played very gently as a background. In order to ensure that beat one is accented each time, ask the children to make a more exaggerated movement as they pull in and back. The accent can be emphasised further by asking a child to tap a drum on the first beat each time. Make sure that the child providing this accompaniment does not stop singing, or there will be a danger of going out of time with the other performers. You might find some children who will also be able to play the two note chime bar accompaniment. Again, make sure that they do not stop singing when performing the instrumental part.

The accompanying movements can be varied. Instead of rowing singly, the children could face each other and, holding each other's hands, could row backwards and forwards as they sing.

Rowing facing each other

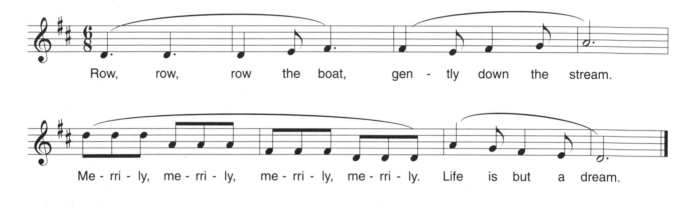

Row, row, row the boat, gen - tly down the stream.

Me - rri - ly, me - rri - ly, me - rri - ly, me - rri - ly. Life is but a dream.

35. MUSIC WHICH DESCRIBES WATER

Draw the children's attention to the fact that there are many pieces which describe water. Play them sections from Ravel's *'Jeux d'eaux'*. Draw their attention to the way that the cascading of the water is reflected in the fast rushes upwards and downwards of the notes. Contrast this by playing them a section from Debussy's *'Reflets dans l'eau'*, where the music is far calmer, like the calmness of deep, slow moving water.

You could reinforce this further by showing the children appropriate pictures when the music is being played. As in other sections, make sure that they are given sufficient time to absorb the music by being able to hear it several times. Also arrange for them to be able to go back to pieces which they have heard at earlier stages. This will help them to build up a repertoire of music with which they are familiar and on which they can draw, not only at this stage but at later stages in their lives.

36. WEE WILLY WINKY

C35–41

Purpose
To give children practice in marking the underlying beat of a song or rhyme via a combination of movements, to help them grasp the notion of up and downward movement as it relates to music, in preparation for future work on pitch development; to give them the experience of improvising appropriate musical sound effects; to help them develop the notion of changing speeds of beat.

Resources
Space for movement; xylophone or glockenspiel; cassette: side 1, track 22; Copymasters 35–41.

Activity
Discuss with the children what time they go to bed. They probably will be unable to give a precise time. Many of them, however, will be able to relate it to the last television programme that they are allowed to watch before getting ready for bed. What happens if they do not go to bed early? How do they feel the next day? How would they like it if someone came checking to see whether they were in bed like Willy Winky?

Teach them the following song with the movements as indicated.

WEE WILLY WINKY

Starting note: C.   Count: 1-2-3-4 1-2-3-4

at a fairly quick pace.

Wee	Willy	Win	ky	runs	through	the	town,
1	2	3	4	1	2		3	4
*	*	*	*	*	*		*	*

Up	stairs and	down	stairs	in his	night	gown.
1	2	3	4	1	2	3	4
↑	↑	↓	↓	↑	↑	↓	↓

Tapping	at the	win	dows	knocking	at the	doors.
1	2	3	4	1	2	3	4
+	+	+	+			

Are the	children	in	their	beds?	It's	past	ten	o'clock.
1	2	3	4		1	2	3	4
!	!	!	!		!	!	!	!

* = Tap on the thigh

↓ = Two arms pushed downwards towards the floor

↑ = Two arms pushed downwards towards the floor.

+ = Fingers of one hand tapping the palm of the other hand

! = Both hands held up in front with 10 fingers showing the time of night

On the words 'upstairs' and 'downstairs', they raise and lower their hands accordingly. This movement can be accompanied by upward and downward glissando slides on the glockenspiel or xylophone. The latter should be upended as before (see p. 38).

Vary the activity by asking the children to mark the beat by moving around the room in time to the beat struck out by yourself, or one of the children, on a drum or tambour.

Focus on the fact that Wee Willy is running. Divide the class into several groups. Give each group of children a different one of the series of the Wee Willy Winky Copymasters (**Copymasters 35–9**) and ask them to describe what type of movements Wee Willy seems to be making. In some instances he is obviously moving very quickly and in others, he is moving extremely slowly.

Ask the children to spread round the room and move to beats struck out by yourself at a range of speeds. Now perform the song with the words changed so that it refers to Willy 'walking', 'dashing', 'crawling', etc. Try out various speeds of beat with the children until you are all satisfied that you have found the appropriate pace for that particular type of movement.

Extension

Look at the pictures of people and vehicles on **Copymaster 40** and ask the children to decide whether they are moving 'Fast' or 'Slow'. Attach the labels from **Copymaster 41** accordingly. When they have grasped this notion, examine the gradations of 'Very fast' (jet fighter) to 'Very slow' (the rock climber).

37. 'WALKING' OR 'RUNNING' MUSIC?

Listen to a variety of pieces of music and discuss whether the music is walking or running? Is it going fast or slow?

Play the children the following pieces: the section from 'Oliver' where Oliver escapes his captors. Draw their attention to the fast pace of the music, the shortness of the notes and the way that it seems to 'run'. Contrast this with Handel's 'Largo', the Second Movement of Beethoven's Seventh Symphony, or 'The Sad Doll'.

38. WHERE AM I? SOUNDS CLUES GAME

C42–4

Purpose
To heighten children's awareness of the sounds produced by the objects in their immediate environment.

Resources
Space for movement; a blindfold; Copymasters 42–4.

Activity
Remind the children of how Wee Willy Winky tapped at the windows and knocked at the doors. Could they tell which sound was which? Use **Copymasters 42–4** as a focus for this discussion.

Arrange for a child to be blindfolded. You, or another child, should then make a sound on an object. The blindfolded child's task is to identify the object on which it has been produced. When the source of the sound has been correctly identified, the child who produced the sound then puts on the blindfold and the game continues. (Later, when the child removes the blindfold, he or she must produce the sound in exactly the same way on the object concerned.)

To reinforce the notion of dynamics, and to extend the activity, the children could also be asked to play and reproduce the sounds at various degrees of loudness and softness.

Extension
When the children are adept at this type of activity, one of them is blindfolded. The others find spaces for themselves in various parts of the room. The blindfolded child calls out a name and the person named has to make a sound, e.g. tapping on the window. On the basis of such sound clues, the blindfolded child has to identify where the other child is in the room.

Another version of this game involves taking the blindfolded child to a particular part of the room which has to be identified on the basis of sound clues produced by the other children.

Several twentieth century composers have made use of the sounds of everyday objects in their compositions. Play some examples of such an approach. The following could be useful: Stockhausens '*Kontakte*' and '*Gesange der Junglinge*', The Beatles song 'I am the Walrus' and 'Two Thousand Light Years from Home' by The Rolling Stones.

39. COPY CAT GAME 1

Purpose
To enable children to extend their experience of composing with body sounds.

Resources
A metronome; a large enough space for movement; cassette: side 1, track 23.

Activity
Lead the children in performing the following 'Copy Cat' game. Perform a series of actions such as: head tap knee tap head tap knee tap, and ask the children to copy you. After an initial testing out period, make sure that the movements are done in time to a regular count, e.g.:

Count in: 1-2 1-2

Thigh	chest	thigh	chest
1	2	1	2

Head	shoulders	head	shoulders
1	2	1	2

Head	shoulders	arms	head	shoulders	arms
1	2	3	1	2	3

Thigh	chest	head	arms	thigh	chest	head	arms
1	2	3	4	1	2	3	4

You can make these movements as simple or as complicated as the children can manage. You could also invite the children themselves to take turns as leaders.

Now start the metronome at a steady rate and practise keeping the movements in time with it. It will probably be best to do this with pairs or small groups at first so that they can hear the tick of the metronome clearly. Practise making sure that the movements accord as closely with the metronome as possible. You could also practise the movements in time with the recording on the cassette.

Extension
When the children have gained a certain amount of confidence in doing this, ask them not only to make the movements but also to make a vocal sound to go with it. Experiment with these vocal sounds, discuss them and then decide which ones to use.

Now you should be in a position to perform your 'musical machine'. The first attempts might not be wonderful but children tend to find this a fascinating activity and are happy to come back to it with new ideas. As with other compositional work, record the result and play it back so that they have some idea of how it sounds.

40. LITTLE MISS MUFFET

C45–7

Purpose
To give children practice in moving in time to the pulse or beat of a song; to give them experience of selecting appropriate instruments to accompany a song and to mark specific events in it; to give them experience of creating a simple composition illustrating the events in a story and of preparing a rudimentary score for this.

Resources
Chime bars, C sharp and D; a range of unpitched instruments; space for movement; cassette: side 1, track 24; Copymasters 45–7.

Activity
Teach the children the following song:

LITTLE MISS MUFFET

Starting note: D.   Count in 1-2 1-2

Little Miss	Muffet
1	2
D	D

Sat on a	tuffet,
1	2
C sharp	C sharp

Eating her	curds and
1	2
D	D

whey _____.	
1	2
C sharp	C sharp

Then came a	spider who
1	2
D	D

Sat down	be -side her and
1	2
C sharp	C sharp

Frightened Miss	Muffet a-
1	2
D	D

way _____.	And
1	2
D sharp	D sharp

Frightened Miss	Muffet a-
1	2
D	D

way _____.	
1	2
D	D

When they are fairly confident in singing this, add the two note accompaniment as indicated.

Now arrange the children so that they are sitting in a circle. One child sits in the middle and acts the part of Miss Muffet. (So that the boys can also take part, the words could, where necessary, be adapted to 'Little John Muffet'.) A second child assumes the role of the spider and takes up position at one side of the circle. The children chant the rhyme, beating on their laps or on

47

the floor in time to the beat of the music. The spider creeps up on Miss Muffet, moving on each beat with very exaggerated gestures. As the spider sits down next to Miss Muffet, she screams and runs away to join the other children in the circle. The spider now becomes Miss Muffet and another child assumes the role of the spider while the song is repeated.

Discuss with the children what sound they could make to frighten Miss Muffet away. (They might suggest shouting, playing a loud clash on the drums or cymbals or a combination of these). Do not reject any of the suggestions. Try each one out to see what the effect is. In that way the children will be learning to recognise that there is a range of possibilities in any composition situation. Let the children discuss the effects of each and decide which to use. They might decide on one sound, a combination of sounds, or on different sounds to be used on successive occasions.

When the children are adept at performing the song, they could slow down on the words 'Then came a spider and sat down beside her' and speed up on the words 'and frightened Miss Muffet away'.

Extension

Spider games

Children find the following games entertaining and they are a useful way of helping to improve their powers of concentration and ability to recognise vocal timbres.

'How many spiders are there behind me?'

The children stand in a circle. One child sits blindfolded in the middle. At a sign from you, several children creep very quietly up behind their blindfolded friend who then has to work out how many people he or she has heard. If a correct guess has been made, the blindfold is passed on to another child and the game is continued.

'Who are the spiders behind me?'

The game is played as above. This time, however, only one child comes out and stands behind Miss Muffet. The latter then has to identify who the spider is from the tone of the spider's voice (spoken or sung).

Composition

Look at **Copymasters 45–7** with the children. Discuss with them how you could tell the story without words, using sounds instead.

Li - ttle Miss Mu - ffet sat on a tu - ffet ea - ting her curds— and

whey.— Then came a spi - der who sat down be - side her and

frigh- tened Miss Mu - ffet a - way.— And frigh- tened Miss Mu - ffet a - way.

In the first picture Miss Muffet is sitting eating. How is she feeling? (Happy). How could you show this? (She might be humming to herself.) Ask them to make up a little tune which she might be humming. In the next picture the spider is approaching. What type of instrument could show this? (Possibly a scraping noise on the guiro.)

Then the spider sits down. Here the children might choose to select the same instrument(s) already used in the sung version above, or they might want to try out other possibilities. The ideas in brackets are no more than suggestions. If you and the children have alternative ideas then you must try them out, discuss and arrange them in the way that you feel sounds best. As with the Humpty Dumpty composition, you might choose to work on different sections of the piece with different groups or on the whole composition with one group.

When the children have tested out their ideas and decided what they want, they can prepare a score. They could do this by drawing the instruments they will use, in the order they appear in the space at the top of the relevant Copymaster. The score could be further refined by asking the children to colour instruments which are to play loudly in one colour, and those which are to play softly in another colour.

41. LISTENING TO SCARY MUSIC

Play the children the theme from the film 'Jaws'. Discuss with them what makes this music scary.

Draw their attention to the low pitch of the notes; the way the beating heart of a frightened person is reflected in the rhythm; the way that silences are used so that the listener does not quite know what to expect next and therefore is made to feel uncomfortable and afraid.

42. LITTLE BO PEEP

Purpose
To give children practice in recognising vocal timbres, both sung and spoken.

Resources
Two chime bars, D and G; cassette: side 1, track 25.

Activity
Teach the children the song.

LITTLE BO PEEP			
Starting note: G. Count in: 1-2 1-2			
Little Bo	Peep has lost her		sheep and
1	2	1	2
G	D	G	D
Doesn't know	whe-re to find		them.
1	2	1	2
G	D	G	D

Leave them a-	lone and	they'll come	home
1	2	1	2
G	D	G	D
Wagging their	tails be	hind	them.
1	2	1	2
G	D	G	G

When the children are fairly confident at singing the song, add the two note accompaniment as indicated.

Now play the following games:

'Which sheep have come home?'
Arrange the children so that they are standing in a circle. One child sits blindfolded in the middle. They all sing the song and walk round in a circle, stepping in time to the beat. At a sign from you, a child creeps up behind the blindfolded child. The last line of the song is sung by the child who has crept up. The blindfolded

child then has to guess, on the basis of the voice, who that child is. (This game could be played by speaking rather than singing. The child who has crept up would then have to be identified on the basis of their speaking voice.) For this game to be successful, the children will need to have heard each other speaking and singing alone on several occasions. For that reason, it might be best to start playing it with small groups of children who know each other well before moving on to playing it with a whole class. (Recording the children's voices and playing them back to the class for them to identify the singer or speaker is another useful complement to this type of activity.)

Extension

'How many sheep behind me?'

The game is played as before. This time several children, at a given sign from you, creep up very softly behind the blindfolded child. The latter has to listen very carefully and work out how many children have come up behind and (on the basis of their voices) who those children are.

'The naughty sheep'

Teach the children the following rhyme which they could either recite or sing:

> Little Bo Peep had naughty sheep,
> They kept on changing places.
> Wherever she looked,
> In tree or nook,
> She always saw different faces.

Ask the children to sit on their chairs in a circle, with one of them sitting blindfolded in the middle. At a sign from you, two children change places very quietly. The blindfolded child tries to catch one of those changing places. A child cannot be caught once they have sat down on the new chair. When a child is caught they have to speak or sing and be identified on the basis of the sound produced. The identified child then becomes the blindfolded one in the middle.

With children who know their numbers, each child could be given a card with a number on it. The blindfolded child calls out two numbers and the children with those two numbers change places. The blindfolded child then tries to catch them and the game continues as before.

Li - ttle Bo - Peep has lost her sheep and does - n't know where to find them.

Leave them a - lone and they'll come home wa - gging their tails be - hind them.

43. COPY CAT GAME 2

C48

Purpose

To give children practice in interpreting a form of notation.

Resources

Copymaster 48; metronome; cassette: side 1, track 26.

Activity

Extend the 'Copy Cat' game in activity 38, so that the children are now involved in producing further patterns, e.g.

1	2		
Clap	snap		
1	2		
Clap	snap		
1	2	3	
Clap	snap	snap	
1	2	3	
Clap	snap	snap	
1	2	3	4
Lap	clap	clap	clap

Count in: 1-2 1-2

1	2	3	4
Lap	clap	clap	clap
1	2		
Stamp	clap		

Here again, the children should be introduced to the pictorial representations of the movements on **Copymaster 48** when they have had practice in copying the movements live.

Make several copies of Copymaster 48, mount them on card and cut them out. Now arrange these in a variety of sequences which the children then have to reproduce in time to the metronome. The class could also respond to the recording on the cassette. When they have gained sufficient confidence in this, let the children themselves decide on the sequences of actions to be reproduced. An extension of this activity involves the production of a sequence of actions by the teacher which the children then have to 'notate' using the photocopied cards.

44. JACK AND JILL

C49–54

Purpose

To give children practice in stepping in time to the underlying beat or pulse of a song; to emphasise the notion of 'down-up' in preparation for later work on pitch development; to give children further experience of differences of speed or tempo; to give them further experience of producing a simple composition illustrating the events in a story; to encourage them to focus on up/down, fast/slow, loud/soft in the production of their musical illustration.

Resources

Cassette: side 1, track 27; chime bars D and G; unpitched instrument, e.g. tambour, claves, glockenspiel, xylophone; space for movement; Copymasters 49–54.

Activity

Teach the children the following song:

JACK AND JILL

Starting note: G. Count in: 1-2 1-2

Jack and	Jill went	up the	hill to
1	2	1	2
G	G	G	G

Fetch a	pail of	wa	ter.
1	2	1	2
D	D	G	G

Jack fell	down and	broke his	crown and
1	2	1	2
D	D	G	G

Jill came	tumbling	af	ter.
1	2	1	2
D	D	G	G

The children hold hands and form a circle. As they sing the tune or chant the words, they move to their left, stepping in time to the beat. On the words 'Jack fell down', all the boys fall to the ground. Then on 'and Jill came tumbling after', the girls do the same. When the children are fairly confident about performing this song, add the two note accompaniment. (Notice that the accompaniment is slightly different for the first line than for the other lines.) A child who is able to move in time to the beat successfully could mark the beat with a tambour or claves.

When the children are adept at performing the first verse, introduce them to the second verse:

Up Jack got and home did trot

As fast as he could make it

There he went to mend his head

With vinegar and brown paper.

Focus particularly on the words 'up' and 'as fast as he could make it'. Reflect this in a faster beat to which the children have to move.

51

Composition

With the children, look at and discuss the six illustrations on **Copymasters 49–54**. In picture one, Jack and Jill are going up the hill. How can they show this in their music? (They could play notes going up in pitch on the xylophone or glockenspiel. They could have two lots of sounds to represent the two children.) How are they moving as they are going up a steep hill? (Slowly, so they should try to play their music slowly.)

Jack is falling down in picture two. How could they show this? (Downward fast slide on the tuned instrument.) What sound will his bucket make? Will it be loud or soft? (A loud clanking sound possibly, which they might choose to illustrate with loud cymbal sounds.) Ask similar questions for picture three. In picture four, Jack is getting up. Will he do this quickly or slowly? (Slowly probably.) How could they show that he is getting up? (With a rise in pitch on one or more of the pitched instruments.)

In picture five, Jack is running home as fast as possible. (Here again, guide the discussion to the need to invent music which moves very quickly.)

How is Jack feeling in the last picture? (Happier, relieved, comforted.) How can this be shown in the music? (With soft, slow music possibly.)

As with previous activities of this type, you might choose to involve the whole class in illustrating each section or have different groups creating different parts. When the children have tried out, discussed and selected the sounds they wish to produce, they could produce a score for each section by drawing the appropriate instruments onto the page. They could use different colours for soft and loud sections and possibly different sizes of instruments for ones which are to be played quickly or slowly. Alternatively, the speeds could be indicated with labels. Again discuss, suggest, try out ideas and encourage the children to arrive at the final decisions.

Record the finished product and discuss it with the children. You could keep the score and return to it at a later date so that the children could have the experience of interpreting it. They could also compare a recording of the second performance with that of the first and discuss the similarities and differences.

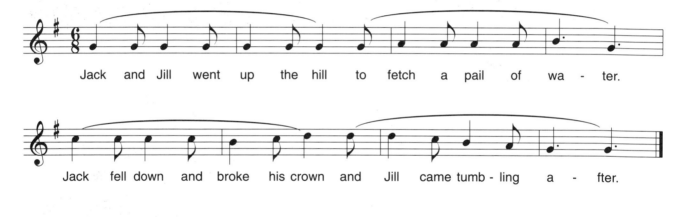

Jack and Jill went up the hill to fetch a pail of wa - ter.

Jack fell down and broke his crown and Jill came tumb - ling a - fter.

45. HIGH AND LOW

C55–8

Purpose

To develop children's concept of high and low in terms of space and to relate this to the development of pitch awareness.

Resources

Space for movement; Copymasters 55–8; the highest sounding (i.e. the smallest chime bar) placed on a table; the lowest sounding (i.e. largest chime bar) placed on the ground.

Activity

In everyday life we use the terms 'high' and 'low' to describe a variety of concepts including differences of volume (Do you have to have that music up so high?) and differences of pitch (That singer can manage some really high notes!). There is evidence that young children can be confused by this interchange of terminology. To avoid this, make sure that you are consistent in your use of terminology. Use 'loud' and 'soft' to refer to differences in volume and 'high' and 'low' for differences of pitch.

Tell the children the fable about the competition between the birds as to which of them could fly the highest. The wren eventually wins because it rides on the back of the eagle. When the eagle gets too tired to fly any higher, the wren takes off and still has the energy to go even higher and win the competition.

Teach the children the following rhyme:

High in the air a little bird flies
Low in the water a big fish lies.

High in the air see the aeroplanes go
Low on the river see the boatmen row.

Discuss with the children what objects or animals, etc. are high or low. Look at the pictures on **Copymasters 55–8** and help the children decide whether they are high or low. Ask them to arrange them into sets of like and unlike objects. You could also produce several sets of the cards and play a pairing game along the same lines as that described in activity 31.

Now ask the children to chant the rhyme you have just taught them. As they do so, play the high chime bar on the beats of the first line and the low chime bar on the beats of the second line of each verse. Individual children could be invited to take over this activity. The children could also emphasise the differences between the two lines by making a high reaching gesture on the beats of the first line and a low reaching gesture on the beats of the second line for each verse. Another way of emphasising the differences would be to ask the children to make as high pitched a sound as possible on the first line and as low pitched a sound as possible on the second.

You might also like to involve the children in helping you make up further rhymes contrasting high and low objects, possibly based on the pictures on the Copymasters.

Reaching high on the beats of the first line

46. LISTENING FOR PITCH

To reinforce the concepts introduced in this section, play the children sections of music which make obvious use of high pitched sounds and low pitched sounds respectively.

For high pitched sounds, play them sections from the following: 'The Bird' from Prokofiev's 'Peter and the Wolf'; 'Dance of the Flutes' from Tchaikovsky's 'Nutcracker Suite'; the opening of Mendlessohn's Violin Concerto.

For low pitched sounds play sections from: 'The Elephant' from Saint-Saëns' 'Carnival of the Animals'; 'Bydlo' from 'Pictures at an Exhibition' by Mussorgsky; 'Tubby the Tuba' and 'Tubby at the Circus' by Kleinsinger and Tripp.

47. TEDDY BEAR, TEDDY BEAR

C59

Purpose
To give children practice in moving in time to the underlying pulse or beat of a song; to reinforce the notion of high and low and up and down by matching appropriate movements to words during the performance of a song; to enable children to convert pitch signs into sounds and vice versa.

Resources
Space for movement, Copymaster 59; cassette: side 1, track 28; chime bars C and G; two further chime bars: the smallest (i.e. the highest pitched) and the largest

(lowest pitched) in the set. These two chime bars should be arranged at different heights: one on the table, the other on the floor so that the differences in pitch are matched by differences in physical height.

Activity
Teach the children the following song.

TEDDY BEAR, TEDDY BEAR
Starting note: G. Count in: 1-2 1-2
Teddy Bear, Teddy Bear turn ar o und. (Turn around)
G   C   G   C   G   C G C

Teddy Bear, Teddy		Bear touch the		ground. (Touch ground)			
G	C	G	C	G	C	G	G

Teddy Bear, Teddy		Bear show your		shoe. (Show shoe)			
G	C	G	C	G	C	G	C

Teddy Bear, Teddy		Bear that		will	do.		
G	C	G	C	G	C	G	C

Teddy Bear, Teddy Bear reach up high. (Reach high)

Teddy Bear, Teddy Bear touch the sky. (Reach higher)

Teddy Bear, Teddy Bear rub your shoe. (Rub shoe)

Teddy Bear, Teddy Bear that will do.

Teddy Bear, Teddy Bear bend down low. (Bend down)

Teddy Bear, Teddy Bear down you go. (Crouch down)

Teddy Bear, Teddy Bear tie your shoe. (Pretend to tie shoe)

Teddy Bear, Teddy Bear that will do.

When the children are able to perform the tune, words and movements fairly fluently, add the chime bar accompaniment as they perform. (Notice that the accompaniment to the second line is slightly different from that of the other lines).

Invite the children to spread themselves around the room and to reach up as high as possible, making as many high shapes as they can. Then ask them to crouch down low. Now draw attention to the high and the low chime bars. Play these in turn. Ensure that the children can see the chime bars, and then ask them to reach up high on the high note and crouch down low on the low note, etc.

When they are able to do this, repeat the activity but this time with the chime bars hidden from view. (This is probably best achieved by asking the children to turn their backs on you.) Individual children can then take turns in playing the chime bars for the others to follow.

Now change the activity slightly so that, instead of converting sounds into signs, the children are asked to convert signs into sounds. Ask one child at a time to come to the chime bars. Stand opposite the child and make a high or low gesture which he or she then has to convert, as appropriate, into a high sound or a low chime bar sound. When they have understood what has to be done, the children themselves can work in pairs on this activity.

This game could be varied further by arranging the children in a circle with one child blindfolded in the middle. The blindfolded child calls out the name of another child. The latter then reaches up high or goes down low. The teacher or another child plays a high chime bar if the movement is a high one and a low chime bar if the movement is a crouching one. On the basis of the sound heard, the blindfolded child then has to decide what type of movement has been made.

Extension

1. Arrange the chime bars as before. This time, however, several children stand in a line making high or low gestures of their own choosing. Another child then has to play the appropriate gesture as you move behind the children from the chime bar player's left to his right. This will be an introduction to the convention of reading music from left to right.

2. Make several copies of **Copymaster 59** and mount them on cards. Arrange these in various orders (e.g. high-low-high; low-low-high, etc.) and ask individual children to convert them into sounds. Conversely, play a series of high and low sounds on the chime bars and ask the children to arrange the cards accordingly.

Reaching up high on the high note

54

This will give the children the opportunity to convert signs into sounds and sounds into signs; both essential activities if they are to become musically literate.

Although several activities have been presented together in this section, the children will need time to develop the concept and also to practise its application.

Therefore, do not try to present all the ideas in one go. Spread them over a period of time but make sure that the children are exposed to them frequently so that they have plenty of practice. This work can, of course, be extended by playing further examples of music which make obvious use of high and low sounds.

48. LONG AND SHORT SOUNDS

Purpose
To draw the children's attention to the fact that sounds vary in duration; to enable them to experiment with ways of producing sounds of different durations on instruments.

Resources
A series of instruments which are capable of producing long and/or short sounds, e.g. triangle, castanet, wood block, chime bar, tambourine, cymbal, guiro, cabasa.

Activity
Arrange the children in a circle, each with a different instrument. Ask each child in turn to play a sound on the instrument concerned. Discuss with the children whether the sound produced was a long sound or a short sound. Arrange the instruments into sets accordingly. You could do this either by placing the actual instruments into separate circles or you could group pictures of the instruments together.

Extension
Repeat the activity as above. This time, encourage the children to find ways in which an instrument which, last time, made a long sound can now be made to produce a short sound.

Experiment with the instruments yourself beforehand so that you can help them if they have difficulties. (A cymbal or chime bar sound, for example, can be made shorter by dampening it, i.e. by putting a finger on it to stop the vibration. A sound on a guiro can be made longer by scraping it very rapidly so that a whole series of tiny sounds combine to produce the effect of a longer one.)

Ask the children to think of the sounds which they hear every day. Which are long sounds and which are short ones? Examples of long sounds might include:

- a bus squealing to a halt
- an aeroplane passing overhead
- a rumble of thunder
- a factory hooter.

Examples of short sounds might include:

- individual drips from a tap
- a door banging shut
- a dog's bark
- the tick of a clock.

Make a list of these for display in the classroom. Extend it as new instances and ideas present themselves.

49. SHORT SHORT LONG

Purpose
To make children aware of the fact that music makes use of combinations of long and short sounds.

Resources
Cassette: side 1, track 29; building blocks of various lengths, both short and long.

Activity
Teach the children the following song:

> SHORT SHORT LONG
>
> Count in: 1-2-3-4 1-2-3
>
>   Short short
>
> Long short short long. Oh,
>
> Listen to my song. It's
>
> Full of little short short notes and
>
> Long   ones.

Discuss with the children the way that, in songs some notes are long and some are short. In this song the words tell us which are which.

Now help the children to arrange the building blocks so that they correspond to the first two lines of the song. Make a diagram of this and display it alongside the other long and short objects. The children could be involved in sorting and matching the relevant pictures.

SOUNDS

Short Short   Long

Short short long short short long. Oh, li - sten to my song. It's

full of li - ttle short short notes and long ones.

50. LISTENING TO LONG AND SHORT SOUNDS

You could reinforce the children's grasp of the concept of long and short in relation to music by playing them sections of the following pieces. Short notes: 'Pizzicato Polka' from 'Sylvia' by Delibes, 'The Minute Waltz' by Chopin, 'Pizzicato' from 'Fantastic Toy Shop' by Rossini/Respighi. Long notes: 'The Great Gate of Kiev' from Mussorgsky's 'Pictures at an Exhibition', Vaughan Williams' 'Sinfonia Antarctica'.

51. RIDE A COCK HORSE

Purpose

To give children practice in moving in time to the underlying pulse or beat of a song; to give them practice in moving at different speeds; to extend their awareness of long and short sounds.

Resources

Space for movement; cassette: side 2, track 1; untuned percussion, e.g. wood blocks, tulip blocks, bells; recording of horses moving at different speeds; chime bars, G, B and C.

Activity

Teach the children the following song:

RIDE A COCK HORSE			
Starting note: C. Count in: 1-2 1-2			
Ride a cock horse to	Ban bu ry	Cross to	
1	2	3	4
C	G	B	G

See a fine la dy	u pon a white horse.		
1	2	3	4
C	G	B	G
Bells on her fingers and	bells on her toes,		
1	2	3	4
C	G	B	G
She shall have mu sic wher e ver she	goes.		
1	2	3	4
C	G	B	C

When the children are familiar with the song, add the accompaniment on the chime bars. (Note how the last line is slightly different from the other three.) The accompaniment could be made more interesting by asking a child to play the hand jingles on the beats. From here, the children could progress to moving in different ways and at different speeds around the room to patterns appropriate for walking, trotting, galloping, etc. You could produce these on tuned as well as untuned instruments.

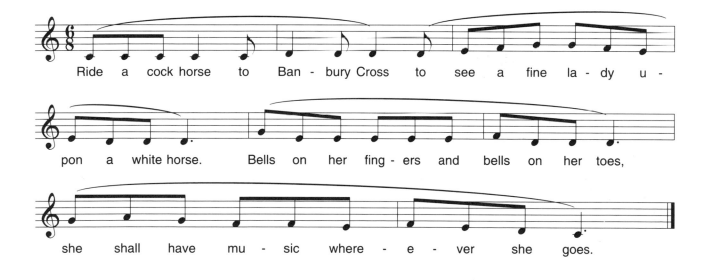

Ride a cock horse to Ban - bury Cross to see a fine la - dy u -

pon a white horse. Bells on her fing - ers and bells on her toes,

she shall have mu - sic where - e - ver she goes.

52. WALKING, GALLOPING, AND TROTTING PATTERNS

C60–62

Purpose

To help you produce walking, galloping and trotting patterns.

Resources

Copymasters 60–62; cassette: side 2, track 2; chime bars D and G.

Activity

1. To produce a trotting accompaniment:

Count: 1–2–3–4 1–2–3–4 at a regular pace. As you do so, play the claves or coconut shells on each count. This can be made more complicated if one person keeps a regular beat with the claves and another shakes hand bells on each count. Instead of playing rhythm sticks, play an alternating pattern on two chime bars, e.g.:

G	D	G	D	G	D	G	D	G	D	G	D, etc.
1	2	3	4	1	2	3	4	1	2	3	4

2. To produce a galloping accompaniment:
Count at a fairly quick pace: 1–2–3 1–2–3 1–2–3 1–2–3, but only strike the rhythm sticks or coconuts on numbers 1 and 3. This creates a LONG short LONG short LONG short LONG pattern.

(Listen to this and and the trotting pattern on the cassette: side 2, track 2.)

When you have gained confidence in producing a galloping rhythm, transfer it to pitched instruments, e.g. two chime bars G and D, could be played as follows:

G		D G		D G		D G		D G		D
1	2	3 1	2	3 1	2	3 1	2	3 1	2	3

When the children are familiar with these patterns, make several copies of the **Copymasters 59–62** and mount them on to cards. Play the recording of various horse movements and ask the children to select the card which corresponds with that movement.

Extension
i. Arrange a series of pictures and as you, or one of the children, points at them, the others move round the room and/or produce an appropriate instrumental rhythmic pattern.
ii. The children could be asked to arrange the pictures of the horses' movements in order of increasing speed.
iii. Work on moving to different speeds and on producing different volumes of sound.

53. HORSES IN MUSIC

Reinforce the work in the preceding activity by playing the children a series of pieces based on horse movements. The children could be encouraged to move to, as well as to listen to, the following pieces – or, at least, sections of them: Bizet, Gallop from *'Jeux d'enfants'*; Elgar, 'Hobby Horse' from Nursery Suite; Schumann, 'Knight on a Hobby Horse' from 'Scenes of Childhood'; Suppé, Overture, from 'The Light Cavalry'; Wagner, 'Ride of the Valkyries'.

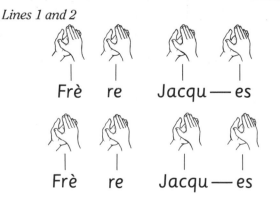

54. GUIDE TO RHYTHMIC NOTATION

Purpose
To enable you, the teacher, to understand a basic method of reading and writing rhythmic patterns.

Resources
The recording of Frère Jacques on cassette: side 2, track 3; a little patience and an ability to tell yourself that you can do it!

Activity
As you will see from the glossary, 'rhythm' is the term which is used to refer to combinations of long and short notes in music. In the remainder of this book, you will be using a simple type of picture and line representation of rhythm which both you and the children should find very easy to use, so long as you approach it gradually.

Listen to the recording of Frère Jacques on the tape and sing along with it. Now sing the song and clap out the rhythm (i.e. each separate note) as you do so. Listen to the tape for guidance. You will notice that, in the first two lines, every note is exactly the same length (and corresponds with the beat). This could be indicated by pictures of hands clapping or by lines as follows:

> FRÈRE JACQUES
>
> Count in: 1-2-3-4 1-2-3-4

Lines 1 and 2

In lines three and four, all the notes are again the same length but, at the end of both lines, there is a silence (known in music as a 'rest'). The silence (rest) in each case is marked either with a wave or by the sign:

Lines 3 and 4

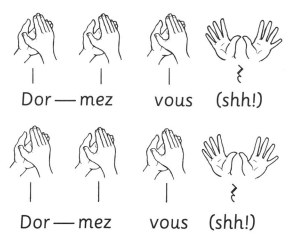

You may have gathered by now that:

– a note which is the same length as a beat is indicated by: |

– two notes to a beat are indicated by: ⌐¬

Look at the following rhythms; try them out and listen to them on the tape:

JINGLE BELLS

i. Count in: 1-2-3-4

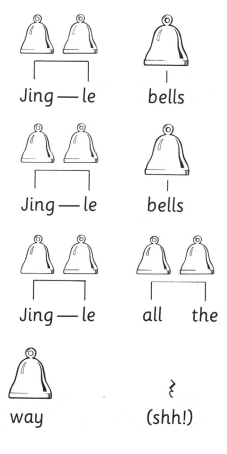

Line five begins with four short notes – two notes per beat. These can be indicated by two groups of small hands or by the sign: ⌐¬ on each beat. The same pattern is found in line six.

Lines 5 and 6

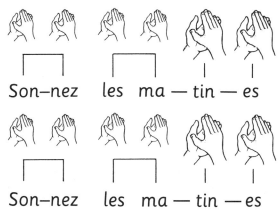

The last two lines are then the same rhythm as lines three and four.

Lines 7 and 8

WALTZING MATILDA

ii. Count in: 1-2-3-4

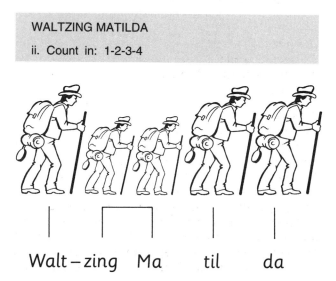

59

UNDER THE SPREADING CHESTNUT TREE

iii. Count in: 1-2-3-4

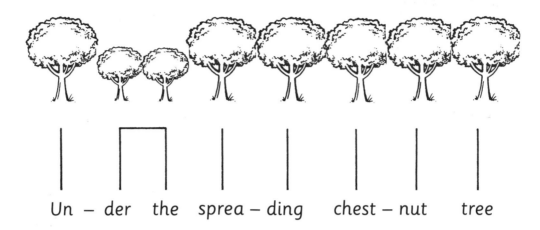

Un – der   the   sprea – ding   chest – nut   tree

The children will eventually learn both of the above types of notation. But, at first they will make use of the picture system where a note corresponding to one beat is indicated by a large picture of a relevant object and shorter notes will be indicated by smaller pictures. The pictures and lines will be used to help you from this point on. But they need not be shown to the children until a little later. They must first have had more experience of reproducing rhythmic patterns from their sound alone, through what is known as 'echo clapping'.

55. ECHO ACTIVITIES

Purpose
To give children practice in reproducing rhythmic patterns performed to them.

Resources
A copy of *Happy Birthday Moon* by Frank Asch, published by Picture Corgi, another story which refers to the notion of echoes; cassette: side 2, track 4.

Activity
Read the children *Happy Birthday Moon*, with its references to echoes.

Now play an echo game. Start by making vocal sounds and body sounds which the children have to echo immediately after you. For example:

Teacher: La la la la
Children: La la la la
Teacher: Clap clap sniff sniff
Children: Clap clap sniff sniff

When they have grasped the idea, tap out a slow, repeated beat pattern. You make your sound on one beat. The children have to respond on the next beat .

Count in: 1-2 1-2			
1	2	1	2
CLAP	(clap)	CLAP	(clap)
1	2	1	2
STAMP	(stamp)	STAMP	(stamp)

1	2	1	2
HELLO	(hello)	HELLO	(hello)
1	2		
WHO'S THERE?	(Who's there?)		
1	2		
WHO'S THERE?	(Who's there?)		

When the children have had some practice on this kind of activity, let them take turns as leaders. Now, in addition to speaking the words, clap their rhythms as well and ask the children to do the same in return.

Some very simple rhythms with their notations are illustrated below to help you prepare this aspect of your work.

Animals

Jack   daw

Food

Pan ——— da

Po ——— lar   bear

Te ——— ddy   bear

Li ——— on

Croc ——— o   dile

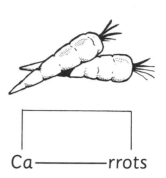

Ca ——— rrots

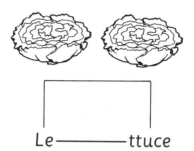

Le ——— ttuce

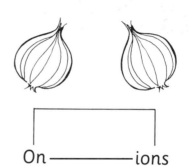

On ——— ions

Corn   flakes

Fish   and   chips

61

Tea

Clothes

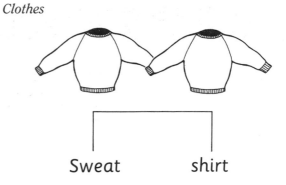

Sweat   shirt

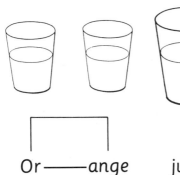

Or——ange   juice

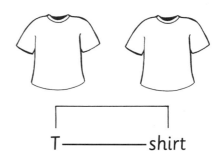

T————shirt

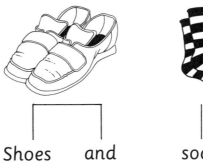

Shoes   and   socks

56. LISTENING TO ECHOES

Seventeenth and eighteenth century European composers make considerable use of echo effects in their music. Therefore it would be well worth exploring such music yourself for useful examples. Three pieces which you might like to draw upon to help develop the notion of musical echoes are: Bach's 'Toccata and Fugue in D minor' and sections from 'The Seasons' by Vivaldi. Another more obvious example of echoing is the echo song from the sound track of Disney's 'Snow White and the Seven Dwarfs'.

57. SWINGING SONG

Purpose

To give children practice in moving in time to the underlying pulse or beat of a song; to give them practice in marking the accents in a song, firstly with movements and then with a simple one note accompaniment on a pitched instrument.

Resources

Cassette: side 2, track 5; chime bar A for you to give the starting note; three chime bars pitched on the note D for individual children to provide the accompaniment. (For the second stage of the activity you will need three chime bars pitched to the notes D, F sharp and A.)

Activity

Read the following poem to the class:

THE SWING

How do you like to go up in a swing,
Up in the air so blue?
Oh, I do think it the pleasantest thing
Ever a child can do!
Up in the air and over the wall,
Till I can see so wide,
Rivers and trees and cattle and all
Over the countryside –
Till I look down on the garden green,
Down on the roof so brown –
Up in the air I go flying again,
Up in the air and down!

By R. L. Stevenson,
from *A Child's Garden of Verses*, Collins.

Discuss the poem with the children. Remind them what it feels like to be on a swing. Remind them also of how, when you push someone on a swing, you have to move regularly and make a stronger movement when you push forward.

Teach the children the following song.

SWINGING SONG
Starting note: A. Count in slowly: 1-2 1-2

Oh, how I	like to	dream and	sing
1	2	1	2
D		D	

When I am riding	on a		swing.
1	2	1	2
D		D	

High and	low,	to	and fro.
1	2	1	2
D		D	

Oh, what a wonderful thing			_____.
1	2	1	2
D		D	

When they are fairly confident at singing the tune and the words, ask them to pretend to be pushing a friend on a swing. Let them practise swaying forwards and backwards as you count regularly:

1	2	1	2	1	2
Forward	back	forward	back	forward	back, etc.

When they are able to do this, ask them to perform the movements as they sing the song.

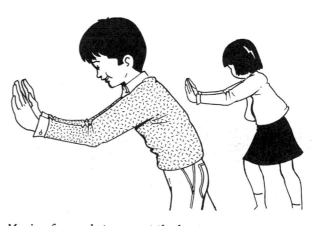

Moving forwards to accent the beat

Oh, how I like— to dream— and sing when I am ri - ding on— a swing.

High— and low, to— and fro. Oh, what a won - der - ful thing.

The next stage is to ask them to put more emphasis on the forward push in order to accent it. This could also be reflected in a slightly louder sound on the corresponding syllable. When they are able to do this effectively, give two or three children at a time a chime bar tuned to D. This time, as those particular children lean forwards, they play the chime bar on the beat.

This could be extended to giving the three children three different pitched chime bars: D, F sharp and A. It is important that the children move as they play the chime bars so that they can translate that physical movement into a sound which is synchronised with the singing.

Discuss with the children the effect of having three notes of different pitches playing at once. Tell them that the term for more than one note being played at at a time is 'chord'. Let them try playing other chords on the chime bars and decide which ones they like best.

58. ECHO CLAPPING

Purpose
To enable children to echo the clapping of rhythms without the aid of words; to enable them to identify words on the basis of their rhythms alone.

Resources
Cassette: side 2, track 6.

Activity
Repeat the approach outlined in activity 55. This time, however, phase out the use of words and rely on the clapped patterns alone. Introduce the activity by listening to the recording.

This can be extended into a guessing game. The children sit in a circle. You start by saying a sentence such as: 'For my breakfast, I like to eat marmalade'. (Clap out the rhythm of 'marmalade' as you say it.) The child on your left then continues by saying a sentence such as the following: 'For my breakfast, I like to eat toast. (The child claps out the rhythm of 'toast'.) When all the children have had a turn at this, tap out a steady beat with your foot, count them in and then repeat the exercise, this time making sure that the children are saying and echoing the name of the food in time to the beat.

For   my   breakfast   I

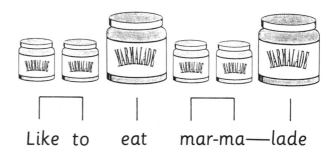

Like   to   eat   mar-ma—lade

The next stage involves omitting the word for the food and simply clapping out the rhythm. The children are then required to echo the rhythm and guess what the food is. There will, of course, be foods which share the same rhythmic pattern. This can be highlighted and used as preparation for later work on rhythm in this book.

Count in 1-2 1-2								
1	2	1		2	1	2	1	2
For	my	break	fast	I	like	to	eat	marma	lade

59. LONDON BRIDGE IS FALLING DOWN

C94

Purpose
To enable children to move in time to the underlying pulse or beat of a song; to give them further practice in marking the accented notes in a song firstly via movements and then by means of simple instrumental accompaniments.

Resources
Space for movement; chime bars C, F and C'; additional chime bars pitched at C for the use of the children; Copymaster 94; cassette: side 2, track 7.

Activity
Teach the children the following song.

LONDON BRIDGE IS FALLING DOWN			
Starting note: C. Count in: 1-2 1-2			
London	Bridge is	falling	down,
1	2	1	2
C'	C	F	F
Falling	down,	falling	down.
1	2	1	2
C	C	F	F

London	Bridge	is	falling	down,
1	2	1	2	
C'	C	F	F	
My	fair	la	dy.	
1	2	1	2	
C'	C	F	F	

Verse 2

Build it up with wood and clay,

Wood and clay, wood and clay.

Build it up with wood and clay,

My fair lady.

See *The Oxford Nursery Rhyme Book* for further verses.

When the children can sing the song fairly confidently, let them march in a circle around the room, stepping in time to the beat. The next stage is for you to add the three note accompaniment as indicated.

From here, the performance can be varied in several ways. For example, two children could form an arch by holding their hands high. The other children march under the arch. The children forming the arch mark the beat by moving their arms rhythmically up and down. Then, on the last beat, they bring their arms further down and capture the child who is going under the arch at that particular moment. The captured child is then out. The winner is the last child to be captured.

Extension

When this has been mastered, give two or three children a chime bar each, pitched on C. They should play these on the first beat each time. Make sure that the children keep marching when they are doing this, otherwise you will have difficulty synchronising the accompaniment with the singing. Do not be surprised if this part of the activity proves too difficult for your class. You could always return to this extension material at a later stage (after activity 69, for example). See **Copymaster 94**.

Lon - don bridge is fa - lling down, fa - lling down, fa - lling down.

Lon - don bridge is fa - lling down, my fair la - dy.

60. MUSIC ABOUT LONDON

Talk to the children about London, its sites and landmarks. London Bridge is only one of these. Another famous landmark is Big Ben. In his *London Symphony*, Vaughan Williams includes the sounds of the chimes of Big Ben. Play the children a section of this and help them to identify the sound when it comes. You could also discuss the rest of the music. Is it loud or soft? Does it move quickly or slowly? Collect a number of pictures of London together, making sure that they show the city at different seasons and in different lights. Let the children tell you which of the pictures reminds them most of the music and what their feelings are when listening to it.

Big Ben

61. CUMULATIVE ECHOING

Purpose
To enable the children to reproduce and identify the rhythmic patterns of a series of words.

Activity
Repeat activity 58. This time, the sentences are extended. You might start by saying: 'For my breakfast, I like to eat toast (clapping the rhythm of 'toast'). The next person then repeats this and adds to it, e.g. 'For my breakfast, I like to eat toast and marmalade' (clapping the rhythm of the last three words.) This game can be extended to include as many words and their rhythms as the children can remember. It can also, of course, be varied to include lists of a different kind, e.g. 'At the zoo, I saw a lion', 'At the zoo, I saw a lion and a giraffe', 'At the zoo, I saw a lion, a giraffe and a polar bear', etc.

At first, it will be best to involve small circles of children so that the lists do not become too long for them to remember. Start the game as before by saying the words as you clap out their rhythms. But then phase out the words and use the rhythms only. As in the earlier section, this can be developed into a guessing game to give children practice in identifying the words being clapped.

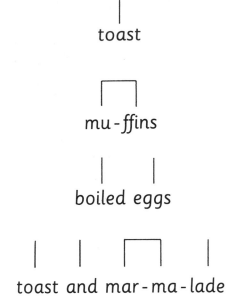

Clapping the rhythm of everyday words

62. LOUD AND SOFT GAMES 1

Purpose
To help develop further children's responsiveness to loud and soft sounds; to develop their ability to perform music at varying volumes; to reinforce the notion of accents in music.

Resources
Pairs of instruments, e.g. two drums, two cymbals, two tambourines; chime bars C, F and G; cassette: side 2, track 8.

Activity
You could start by recapping an earlier activity such as activities 39, 43 or 55. Arrange the children so that they are sitting in a circle with their eyes closed. They all sit as still and as quietly as possible and listen to the sounds which they can hear around them. After a few minutes, ask them to open their eyes. Discuss the sounds they heard. Make a note of the sounds either by small drawings on the board or by making labels as they talk. The children now go back over the sounds and decide which sounds are loud and which ones are soft.

Next, arrange the children in a circle and lead them in a body sound echoing game. This time emphasise the need to reproduce a sound not only in terms of its timbre but also in terms of its volume.

Now develop the activity to involve instruments. Arrange the children in pairs. Give both children within each pair identical instruments. Ask one child to act as leader and to play loudly or softly on the instrument. The second child then has to respond at the same volume. Each child has a turn as a leader.

This game can be extended by asking the second child to reproduce not only the volume but also the precise way of playing on the instrument.

Teach the children the following song, making sure that the first verse is sung loudly and the second is sung softly:

WE CAN SING SOME LOUD SONGS							
Starting note: E. Count in: 1-2-3-4 1-2-3-4							
We	can	sing	some	loud	sounds, tra-la	la-la	laa_____.
1	2	3	4	1	2	3	4
C		C		C		C	
We	can	sing	some	loud	sounds, tra-la-la-la-laa_____.		
1	2	3	4	1	2	3	4
G		G		G		G	
We	can	sing	some	loud	sounds, tra-la	la-la	laa_____.
1	2	3	4	1	2	3	4
C		C		C		C	

We	can	sing	some	loud	sounds,	tra-la	la-la	laa_____.
1	2		3	4	1	2	3	4
F			F		F		C	

We	can	sing	some	soft	sounds,	tra-la	la-la	laa_____.
1	2		3	4	1	2	3	4
C			C		C		C	

We	can	sing	some	soft	sounds,	tra-la	la-la	laa_____.
1	2		3	4				
C			C		C		C	

We	can	sing	some	soft	sounds,	tra-la	la-la	laa_____.
1	2		3	4	1	2	3	4
F			F		F		F	

We	can	sing	some	soft	sounds,	tra-la	la-la	laa_____.
1	2		3	4	1	2	3	4
G			G		G		G	

When the children are fairly confident at performing the song, add the chime bar accompaniment. Point out to the class that you will be playing the chime bar notes on the accented beats.

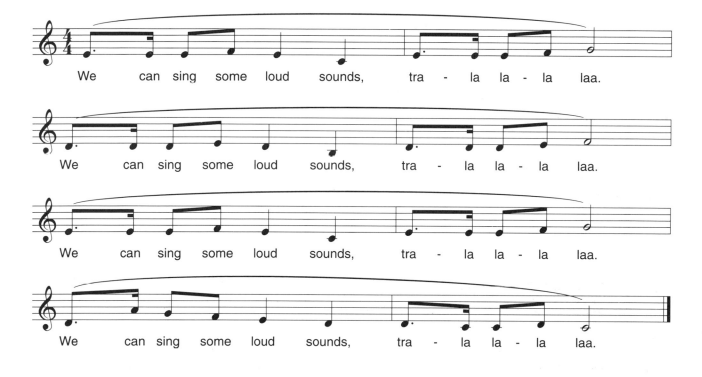

We can sing some loud sounds, tra - la la - la laa.

We can sing some loud sounds, tra - la la la - la laa.

We can sing some loud sounds, tra - la la - la laa.

We can sing some loud sounds, tra - la la - la laa.

63. LISTENING TO ACCENTED BEATS

Play the children a section of a Strauss waltz. Draw their attention to the way that some notes are accented regularly. When they have listened to the piece several times and know it well, they might even be able to mark the accented beats through movements as they listen.

The accented notes in the waltz are predictable after a while. In Haydn's Surprise Symphony, however, they are unexpected. Play them a section of the second movement so that they can hear the effect of unexpected accents.

64. LOUD AND SOFT GAMES 2

Purpose

To give children practice in performing contrasts of loud and soft sounds.

Resources

Pairs of instruments as in the previous section; chime bars C, F and G; cassette: side 2, track 9.

Activity

Teach the children the following additional verse to the song learnt in activity 62. Make sure that a reference to a loud sound is sung loudly and a reference to a soft sound is sung softly. Take time to help the children to produce the appropriate volume in each case.

WE CAN SING BOTH LOUD AND SOFT

Starting note: E.   Count in: 1-2-3-4 1-2-3-4

We can sing both loud and soft,   tra-la la-la laa_____.

1	2	3	4	1	2	3	4
C		C		C		C	

We can sing both loud and soft,   tra-la la-la laa_____.

1	2	3	4	1	2	3	4
G		G		G		G	

We can sing both loud and soft,   tra-la la-la laa_____.

C		C		C	C		
1	2	3	4	1	2	3	4

We can sing both loud and soft,   tra-la la-la laa_____.

F		F		F		F	
1	2	3	4	1	2	3	4

This could be extended by changing the volume indications. For example, the first line could read: 'We can sing both soft and loud.'

You could involve the children in deciding on a whole range of possibilities. Do not expect to be able to do this all in one go. You can always return to the activity periodically and vary the activity each time.

The instrument copying game from activity 48 can also be extended in a variety of ways. For example, a loud sound produced by the leader could be answered by a soft sound and vice versa.

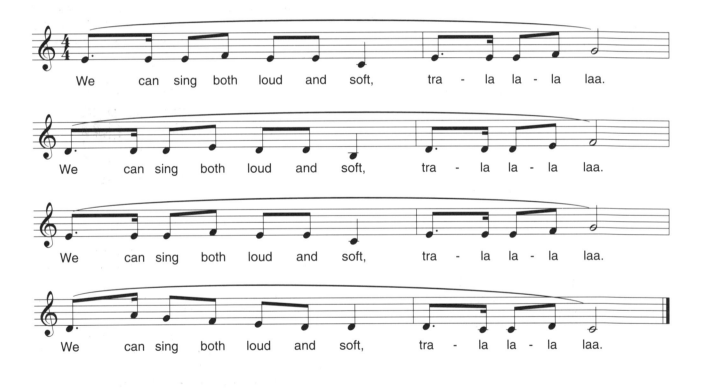

We can sing both loud and soft, tra - la la - la laa.
We can sing both loud and soft, tra - la la - la laa.
We can sing both loud and soft, tra - la la - la laa.
We can sing both loud and soft, tra - la la - la laa.

65. LISTENING FOR CONTRASTS IN VOLUME

Listen to pieces incorporating clear contrasts in volume, e.g. Stravinsky's 'Rite of Spring' Suite. Draw their attention to the soft opening on the bassoon and the way that this contrasts with the loud, frenzied dance that follows it.

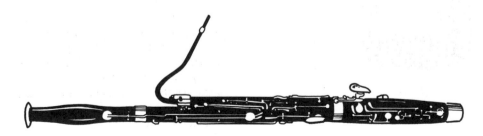

66. RHYTHM PICTURE NOTATION

C63, 64

Purpose

To introduce children to a method of notating rhythms through pictures; to give them further practice in identifying like and unlike rhythms and classifying them accordingly; to give them practice in performing rhythmic patterns at varying volumes.

Resources

Copymasters 63 and 64; cassette: side 2, track 10.

Activity

Start by playing the rhythmic echo games already encountered in earlier sections. This time, however, concentrate on ensuring that the children reproduce the patterns at the appropriate volume. Therefore if you clap out a pattern very softly, the children should repeat it softly. If you clap loudly, then the echo must also be loud, etc.

You could vary the game by using sentences such as the following: For tea, I like to eat ___' or 'When I lay the table, I put on ___'.

As with the previous games, the children add to these sentences by saying and clapping the rhythms of appropriate words. Now focus more specifically on the sound patterns of the words. Some words, such as jam, tea and knife, have one sound. Other words, such as jelly, honey and lemon, have two sounds and some have several sounds some of which are short and some of which are long (e.g. marmalade, lemonade, etc.).

toast

jam

Single sounds can be notated with one picture

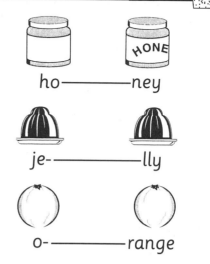

ho———ney

je-————lly

o-————range

Two short sounds are notated using two small pictures

When words have combinations of short and long sounds, we can use combinations of small and large pictures, e.g. lemonade, orangeade, margarine, etc.

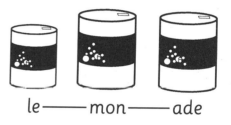

le——mon——ade

Now involve the children in:

i. clapping out the rhythms of a whole range of words;
ii. deciding what pattern of long or short notes they consist of;
iii. arranging the notation patterns appropriately, using the Copymaster available.

You could start with a random selection of words. Then, at a later point, the children could be involved in classifying like and unlike words.

Copymasters 63 and **64** are meant as a start. You can obviously add both to the words and to the pictures now that you have understood the underlying principle. These pictures could form the basis of a classroom display, to which new pictures could be added from time to time.

You could also devise a series of further games based on word rhythms. For example, the children could go shopping and order things using the rhythms of the words. They could pretend to lay the table and tap out the rhythms of the cutlery, crockery and food. On hearing these patterns, another child or group of children could then arrange the picture notations appropriately. In this way, the children will be involved in the two-fold process of converting sounds in to signs and signs into sounds; both essential processes in developing musical literacy.

67. MORE MAGIC MOVEMENTS

Purpose
To give children further practice in responding to loud and soft sounds; to give them further practice in identifying and responding to instruments of varying timbres.

Resources
Space for movement; a small number of instruments of varying timbres, e.g. bongos, triangle, tambourine, castanet, chime bar.

Activity
Let the children handle the instruments available and experiment with them so that they become familiar with the sounds that each instrument produces. Then ask them to spread around the room ready to play a variation on the Simon Says game. Choose one instrument (e.g. tambourine) and explain that they

must only respond to a spoken command such as 'Lift your arm' if the tambourine, rather than one of the other instruments, is playing. Give them practice in this activity.

Next, explain that they must only respond to a spoken command if the tambourine is playing softly. You could practise this by playing the game using the tambourine only. When the children have grasped this, tell them again that they must only respond to a command if the tambourine is playing softly. This time, however, you will also be using other instruments as well as the tambourine.

Obviously there can be many permutations of this game and it is one that the children will enjoy returning to and making more complicated each time. They will also want to assume leadership in this type of game at an early stage.

68. ZADOK THE PRIEST

This activity will give children practice in listening to a piece of music and identifying volume changes within it.

Listen to the opening of Handel's 'Zadok, the Priest'. Draw the children's attention to the way that the music starts quietly and then builds up gradually in volume until the choir enters on a full, loud sound.

Remind the children that this piece has been sung at every coronation since the coronation of George II in 1727.

69. FOLLOW MY LEADER'S ACCENTS

Purpose
To give children further practice in accenting the beats within a song.

Resources
Space for movement; a variety of unpitched percussion instruments; chime bars D and A; cassette: side 2, track 11.

Activity
Teach the children the following song:

MARK THE ACCENT

Starting note: D.   Count in: 1-2-3-4 1-2-3-4

Mark	the	acc	ent,
1	2	3	4
D	A	D	A

Mark	the	acc	ent.
1	2	3	4
D	A	D	A
With	a	clap____	
1	2	3	4
D	A	D	A
With	a	clap____.	
1	2	3	4
D	A	D	A
Come and	mark the	acc	ent.
1	2	3	4
D	A	D	A

Come and	mark the	acc	ent
1	2	3	4
D	A	D	A
With	a	clap____.	
1	2	3	4
D	A	D	A
With	a	clap____.	
1	2	3	4
D	A	D	A

When they have learnt the tune and the words, mark the accented beats (i.e. beats 1 and 3) with a clap. From here, you could vary the text and the movements in a variety of ways, e.g. by marking the accents with a jump, hop, skip or a stamp or any other ideas suggested by yourself and the children. The tune could also be sung and the accents marked as you move round the room. At a later stage, individual children could take up the leadership. You could then provide the two note ostinato accompaniment indicated. Later still, some of the children could accompany their own accented movements with a sound on an unpitched percussion instrument. Experiment with various combinations of percussion sounds and, after discussion with the children, decide which combination to use.

Marking the accents with a stamp

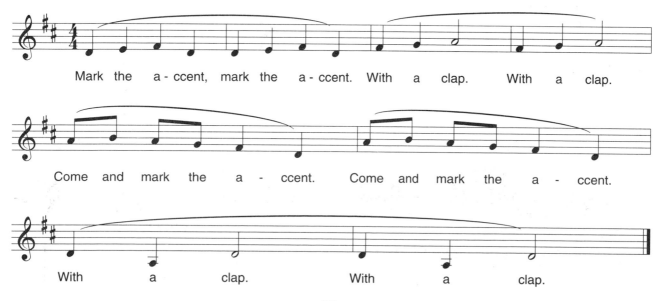

Mark the a-ccent, mark the a-ccent. With a clap. With a clap.

Come and mark the a-ccent. Come and mark the a-ccent.

With a clap. With a clap.

71

70. WHO IS MAKING THE LOUDEST SOUND?

Purpose
To develop further the children's ability to perform, respond to and identify differences between loud and soft.

Resources
The cassette track of any song which the children have already learnt

Activity
Seat the children in a circle and sing through and practise any song which they already know well. Sing the song through with them at various volumes, sometimes loud, sometimes soft and sometimes at a moderate volume. When they have done this successfully, ask one child to sit blindfolded in the centre of the circle. Now ask the rest of the class to sing the song again. This time, all except one child should sing the song softly. One child, chosen by yourself, should sing it loudly. The blindfolded child listens very carefully and has to identify who is singing the loudest.

Who is singing the loudest?

71. LISTENING TO SOLOISTS

Play the children examples of the following: a soloist, singing against a choir; a soloist singing against instrumental backing; a solo instrument playing against an orchestra and/or pop group.

Draw the children's attention to the way that occasionally the soloist blends in with the other performers. At other times, the 'backing' group performs far more quietly, so that the sound of the soloist stands out and can be clearly heard.

72. THE GRAND OLD DUKE OF YORK

Purpose
To introduce children to the notion of three pitch levels; to give them further experience of marking the pulse of a song through movement.

Resources
Cassette: side 2, track 12; space for movement; drum; three chime bars: the smallest (i.e. highest pitched) chime bar that you have, the largest (i.e. lowest pitched)

chime bar and a chime bar of middle size and of middle pitch. Arrange these on three levels as follows: the highest pitched chime bar on a table; the middle pitched chime bar on a chair and the lowest pitched chime bar on the floor. In addition to the above chime bars, you will need a chime bar D for the starting note.

Activity

Teach the children the song:

When they were only		half way	up they were
1	2	1	2
Neither	up	nor	down_____.
1	2	1	2

THE GRAND OLD DUKE OF YORK			
Starting note: D. Because the first note starts on beat 2 count in 1-2-1- The			
			The
1	2	1	2
Grand old	Duke of	York,	he
1	2	1	2
Had ten	thou sand	men.	He
1	2	1	2
Marched them up	to the	top of the hill and	
1	2	1	2
Marched them	down	a gain.	And
1	2	1	2
When they were up they were	up	and	
1	2	1	2
When they were down they were down	and		
1	2	1	2

When the children are fairly confident at singing the tune and the words, ask them to march around the room in time to the beat. Mark the beat with a beat on the drum. After you have introduced the idea, let the children take turns in playing the drum. Ask them to do this while they are moving around so that synchronisation is ensured.

The next stage is to ask the children to spread out and stand at various points around the room. Now perform the song again. This time, on the words 'And when they were up they were up', the children should reach up high. On the words 'And when they were down they were down', they should crouch down low. On the words 'And when they were only half way up' they should stretch their arms out in front of them at waist level. They could maintain this position for the rest of the song or they could reach up and crouch down again as the corresponding words are sung.

This activity could be developed in various ways. For example you, or one of the children, could mark out the beat on a drum again while the group performs. The children could also march on the spot as they perform the actions.

You might also discuss with them what other instruments could be used to mark the beat which would also maintain the military flavour of the sound.

73

(You might decide to use a cymbal as well as the drum, for example.)

When the children are confident in performing the above actions, you should match the children's movements by playing the appropriately-pitched chime bar. Thus, as they reach up, the highest pitched chime bar (on the table) should be struck. As they crouch down, you should sound the lowest pitched chime bar (on the floor) and, as they reach out in front, you should play the middle pitched chime bar (on the chair).

After a while, you could ask the children to take turns in playing the chime bars in this way. Make sure that, as you introduce the children to this part of the activity, you draw their attention to the correspondence between the position of the chime bars and the references to physical levels.

73. MORE PICTURE NOTATION

C65
–7

Purpose

To give children experience of applying picture notation to more extended sentences and rhymes; to give them further practice in converting sounds into signs and signs into sounds using picture notation.

Resources

Copymasters 65–7; cassette: side 2, track 13.

Activity

Arrange the children in a circle with you as part of that circle. Say the following sentence to them, introducing it with a regular beat.

Count in: 1-2-3-4-1-2-3-4

I like boiled eggs

12 3   4

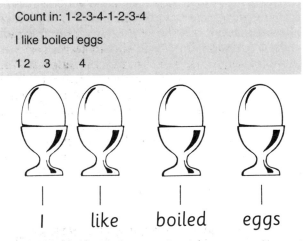

I   like   boiled   eggs

Ask the children to repeat it with you, tapping out the rhythm regularly on their laps as they speak it. Now ask them how many sounds words there were to each beat (one sound per beat). Remind them that we use a large picture of an object every time there is one sound to a beat. Therefore, if we are going to use pictures of eggs, there will be one large egg for each beat. Show them how this is notated on **Copymasters 65–7**.

Now repeat the exercise with a new sentence:

I like fish and chips

12 3   4

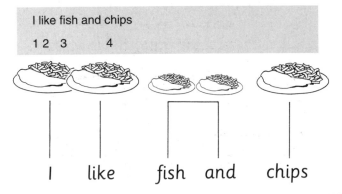

I   like   fish and   chips

Again make sure that you count in regularly and that the children also maintain the beat with regular tapping on their laps.

Count in: 1-2-3-4-1-2-3-4

I like porridge

12   3   4

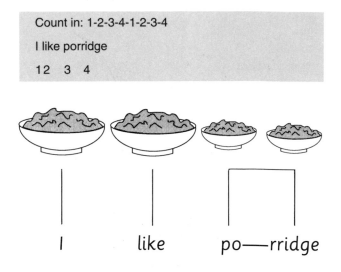

I   like   po——rridge

Through discussion, draw the children's attention to the fact that this time the third beat has two sounds. Therefore there will be a need to use two small pictures on that beat. The others will continue to have one large picture each. Show them the example on the Copymaster. Then let them perform it with you, this time tapping out the long and the short notes (i.e. the rhythm of the sentence rather than the underlying beat).

Now present them with the following sentences and pictures. In doing so, try to ensure variety. You could present each one, as in the above examples, by:

- speaking out the rhythmic pattern
- discussing it
- showing the children the pictures
- clapping out the rhythmic pattern of long and short notes.

Another approach would be to present them with both the pictures and the words at the same time.

A further alternative would be to present them with the pictures only and let them work out which are the long sounds and which are the short sounds before clapping them out.

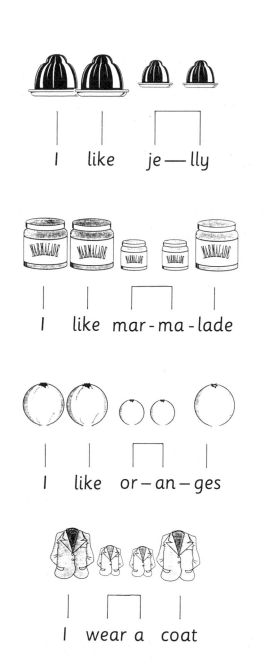

I like je — lly

I like mar - ma - lade

I like or - an - ges

I wear a coat

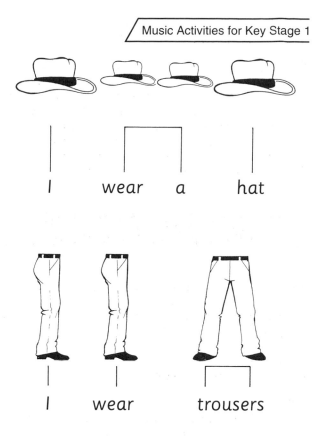

I wear a hat

I wear trousers

As with previous activities in this book, do not expect to be able to cover all these ideas at once. Come back to them for short periods at regular intervals in order to give time to develop and consolidate the skills involved.

Again, do not feel that you have to keep slavishly to the examples given here. Once you have understood the principle, you could devise your own sentences – either yourself or with the help of the children and produce your own pictures to notate the rhythms. If you do choose to create your own, it is worth remembering that it makes it easier for the children if some parts of the sentences are already familiar to them and recur from one example to the other. You will see that this approach has been used above.

74. SOMETIMES I REACH UP HIGH

Purpose
To give children further practice in identifying and responding to notes at three different pitch levels.

Resources
Cassette: side 2, track 14; space for movement; three chime bars: the lowest sounding C that you have, the highest sounding C and a G pitched at a level between the other two notes. Arrange the chime bars so that the highest pitched bar is on a table, the lowest pitched one on the floor and the middle pitched bar is on a chair (as in activity 72).

Activity
Teach the class the following song.

SOMETIMES I REACH UP HIGH

Starting note: G. Count: 1-2 1-Some

				Some
1	2	1	2	
Times I	reach up	high____.	Some	
1	2	1	2	
Times I	go down	low____.	Some	
1	2	1	2	
Times I'm in the	mid	dle.		
1	2	1	2	
Now where shall I	go?____			
1	2	1	2	

75

When the children are adept at this, ask them to make high movements, low movements and middle ones to correspond to the references in the song.

The next stage is to ask the children to spread around the room facing you and in such a way that they can clearly see the chime bars on the three different levels. Play each of the chime bars in turn and ask the children to make corresponding movements high, middle or low. After a while you could mix these up. You could also invite individual children to lead the activity. Draw attention to the fact that a sound is of a low, high or middle pitch and make sure that the children are listening to the sound as well as watching the position of the chime bars as they make their movements.

When they have had practice in doing this, ask them to turn their backs on you as you play the various chime bars. Now they will have to rely on the pitch alone if they are to make the appropriate movement.

The next stage is to ask the children to perform the song again. This time the three chime bars should be out of sight. As soon as the last note has ended, play one of the three chime bars and ask the children to make the appropriate physical response. As before, the children could take turns in leading this activity.

There is a considerable amount of work in this activity. Do not attempt to work through it all at once. The children will need time to absorb each stage. Therefore, as with many of the other activities in the book, this is one to which you should return at regular intervals making sure that each time there is consolidation of existing skills and an opportunity to develop them further.

Identifying high, low and middle pitch sounds

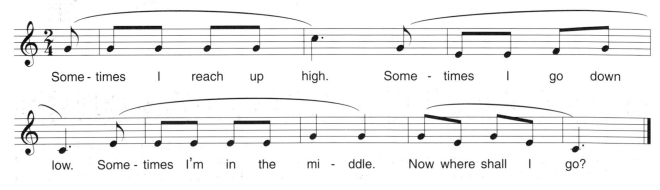

Some - times I reach up high. Some - times I go down

low. Some - times I'm in the mi - ddle. Now where shall I go?

75. CONSOLIDATING PITCH DISCRIMINATION

Purpose
To give children practice in determining whether the sounds which they hear around them are high pitched, low pitched, middle pitched or have no clearly identifiable pitch.

Resources
Tape recordings of a variety of high, middle and low pitched sounds from everyday life. Try to ensure that these form part of the sound environment of your particular pupils.

Activity

Remind the children of how you have been listening to high pitched, low pitched and middle pitched sounds. Now discuss with them the pitch of types of sounds in the world around us.

● *High pitched sounds:* referee's whistle, whistling kettle boiling, sparrows chirping, black birds singing, telephone ringing.
● *Middle pitched sounds:* woman talking, fan whirring, cat purring
● *Low pitched sounds:* someone snoring, fog horn, ship's siren, dog growling, lorry rumbling.

There are many variations on these examples. A cat, for instance, might have a very low purr and some telephones might have a medium pitched ring. This is why it is important to draw on actual examples in the children's direct environment and to listen to them, not simply describe them.

You could make lists of your classifications of the sounds and illustrate them. These could form the basis of a classroom display, to which the children could add new examples from time to time.

There will also be sounds which are difficult to classify into any of these pitch categories. These could also be listed and illustrated.

76. WHO AM I? VOLUME CLUES

Purpose

To give children further practice in performing and discriminating between loud and soft sounds.

Resources

Three or four pitched and unpitched instruments.

Activity

Arrange the children so that they are sitting in a circle. One child is blindfolded and sits in the middle. Three or four children have instruments in front of them. At a sign from you another child goes and stands behind the blindfolded child. The latter now has to guess who is there by asking a number of questions, for example, 'Are you a boy?' 'Do you have black hair?', etc. These questions can be asked to simple two or three note 'tunes'. The instrumentalists respond by playing loudly if the answer is 'yes' and softly if the answer is 'no', etc. When the child has been correctly identified he or she then assumes the blindfold and the game continues. To ensure that everyone is involved, the composition of the group of instrumentalists should be varied from time to time.

77. WHO AM I? RHYTHM CLUES

Purpose

To enable children to recognise and respond to the rhythmic patterns of their own and other children's names.

Resources

Space for movement; tambour or other unpitched percussion instrument.

Activity

Play the 'Simon Says' game giving instructions such as 'Jenny, touch your nose', 'Habib, stand up'. But the children must only respond if they hear the rhythms of their own names being beaten out on the tambour immediately after the instruction has been given. A child who moves when she or he should not is out. The last one out is the winner.

Extension

The children could make large and small drawings of themselves and arrange them into the rhythm pattern for their names. Thus 'Jonathan' would have two small pictures followed by a large one. Kristel would have two small pictures, etc. These drawings could become part of a classroom display on a theme such as 'Ourselves'.

78. POSITIONING CHIME BARS

Purpose
To give children practice in converting signs into musical sounds using three pitch levels.

Resources
This is an extension of the work outlined in activity 74 above, therefore the resources will be the same.

Activity
In the earlier section, the children were involved in converting sounds into signs. The next stage is to involve them in converting signs into sounds. To do this, ask a group of three children to stand in a line with their arms raised, or crouching down or maintaining a 'middle' position. Another child (the performer) should now decide which pitches are being represented. When this has been done, walk behind the three children, from the performer's left to their right. As you pass a particular child, the performer must convert the gesture being made by that child into a low, middle or high sound.

A wide variety of patterns can be presented and also longer ones involving more 'human notes'. Gradually, the class itself can take responsibility for leading the activity.

79. ORANGES AND LEMONS

C68 –71

Purpose
To give children further practice in moving in time to the underlying pulse or beat of a song; to give them practice in marking the accented notes in a song, firstly via movements and then by means of a simple instrumental accompaniment; to give them practice in reading familiar rhythmic patterns from picture notation.

Resources
Space for movement; chime bars C, F and high C' arranged as shown; further chime bars pitched at C for the children to use; Copymasters 68–71; cassette: side 2, track 15.

Activity
Teach the children the song.

ORANGES AND LEMONS

Starting note: C.   Count in: 1-2-3 1-2-3

Oranges and lemons say the

1	2	3	1	2	3
C'	C	C	F	C'	C'

Bells of Saint Clements.

1	2	3	1	2	3
C'	C	C	F	C	C

Further verses

Bull's eyes and targets
Say the bells of Saint Margarets.

Pokers and tongs
Say the bells of Saint Johns.

Two sticks and apple
Say the bells at Whitechapel.

When the children can sing the song fairly confidently, let them march in a circle around the room to the beat of the music. Next add the accompaniment as shown. Two children now form an arch by holding hands. They mark the beat by moving their arms up and down in time to the music. As with 'London Bridge' (activity 59), this can be developed into a catching game with the winner being the last child to be caught.

When they are able to do this successfully, ask the children to perform the song, this time marking the beat by marching on the spot. Note that unlike 'London Bridge', the first beat is not consistently on the same foot because the beats are arranged in groups of three. Ask half the children to count the beats regularly: 1-2-3 1-2-3.

Next, give one or two of the children chime bars pitched on C. As they count out the beats, they should play on each first beat. Now repeat the game and performance as before but this time with the additional chime bars providing an extra element in the accompaniment.

In addition to (or instead of) the chime bars, you could invite the children to provide bell sounds on the first beat. Try out and discuss different types of bell sounds for each of the churches mentioned. For example, you could use a large deep sounding cow bell for one church and a smaller, higher sounding cow bell for another. Alternatively, you might decide to have a different pitched C chime bar for each church. Try out several alternatives and involve the children in discussing the various effects and making decisions.

Extension
Involve the children in making a list of all the bells on public buildings and churches in the vicinity of the school. Classify these into low, middle or high sounds and experiment with ways to reproduce these sounds with a variety of ringing instruments. Listen to other familiar bell sounds such as the sound of Big Ben at the beginning of news broadcasts.

Using **Copymaster 68** help the children to read the rhythmic notation for 'Oranges and lemons'.

From here, you could progress to further notation work. Clap out the opening rhythm of the song. Then, with the aid of several copies of **Copymasters 69–71** notate the rhythm.

You could also discuss with the children whether the sounds go down or up and put the cards at three heights i.e. Oran (high) ges (middle) and (high) Le (middle) mons (low). In this way you will be helping the children to begin to notate pitches, as well as rhythms, with the aid of the pictures. By using oranges and lemons, rather then bells, you will also be emphasising that it is the *size* and *arrangement* of objects, not what they represent which are important.

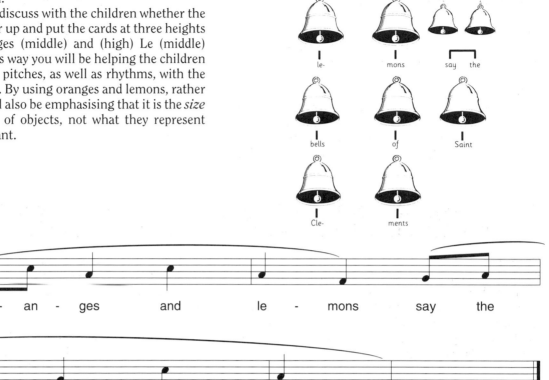

80. MUSIC BASED ON BELLS

Play the children a variety of pieces based on bell sounds. The following would be useful for this: Debussy's 'The Sunken Cathedral'; Tchaikovsky's 'Dance of the Sugar Plum Fairy'; final section of the *1812 Overture*.

Draw the children's attention to the fact that Debussy uses a piano to give the impression of the sounds of the bells of a cathedral which has been engulfed by water. The sound is rather muffled, eerie and indistinct. This is very different from the bright clear sounds of Tchaikovsky's piece.

81. PICTURE NOTATION FOR EXTENDED RHYMES

C72 –6

Purpose
To give children further practice in using picture rhythm notation in relation to more extended rhymes.

Resources
Copymasters 72–6; cassette: side 2, track 16.

Activity
The method of presentation here is very similar to the approach already encountered in activity 73 above and you are advised to remind yourself of that before moving on to these new activities. See **Copymasters 72–6** for picture notation.

Tap out a regular beat on your lap and ask the

children to copy you. When this has been established, count in: 1-2-3-4 1-2-3-4 and say the following rhyme:

1

Rain		rain		go	a	way
1		2		3		4
Come	a	gain	an	o	ther	day
1		2		3		4

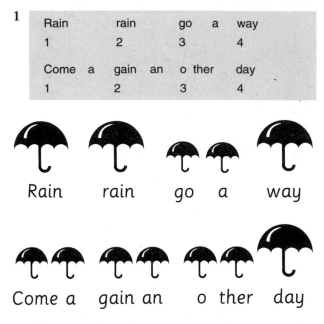

Rain   rain   go   a   way

Come a   gain an   o ther   day

Invite the children to join with you in chanting the rhyme while still maintaining a steady beat. When they have done this successfully, discuss with them which sounds were the same length as the beat and which ones were quicker. Then show them the pictures – large umbrellas for the longer sounds and groups of two small umbrellas for the shorter sounds. At this point, the children can join with you in clapping out the long and short note patterns which constitute the rhythm of the rhymes. You can now apply a similar approach to the following rhymes. You could start by including the words on the copymasters, then blanking them out.

2

Count in: 1-2-3-4 1-2-3-4			
Step	step	step in	line
1	2	3	4
We	are	sol diers	fine
1	2	3	4

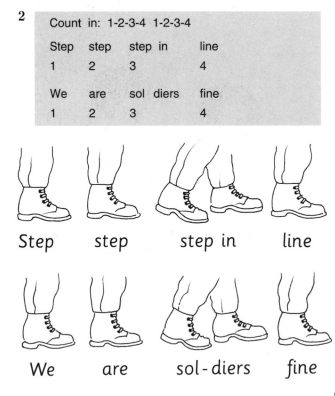

Step   step   step in   line

We   are   sol - diers   fine

3

Count in: 1-2-3-4 1-2-3-4			
Who	stole my	bis	cuit?
1	2	3	4
Ask Je	mi ma	Bris	kett
1	2	3	4

NICE   NICE NICE   NICE   NICE

Who   stole my   bis – cuit?

NICE NICE NICE NICE   NICE   NICE

Ask Je - mi - ma Bris — kett

4

Count in: 1-2-3-4 1-2-3-4			
Where	has my	litt - le	
1	2	3	4
Di	no saur	gone to?	
1	2	3	4

Where   has   my   li——ttle

Di—no—saur   gone   to?

5

Count in: 1-2 1-2	
Little	Mouse
1	2
Little	Mouse
1	2
May we	come to
1	2
See your house?	
1	2

Li-ttle mouse li-ttle mouse

May we come to see your house?

As in the earlier section, you could involve the children in making up their own rhymes and in producing appropriate pictures to illustrate these.

82. DIDDLE DIDDLE DUMPLING, MY SON JOHN

Purpose

To give children further practice in marking the accented beats in a song through movement; to give children practice in adding simple pitched and unpitched percussion accompaniments to a song.

Resources

Space for movement; cassette: side 2, track 17; chime bars, F and high F'; a range of unpitched percussion organised in two categories, e.g. wooden and metal, wooden and skin, metal and skin. (The precise categories will depend on the type and number of instruments which you have available in your classroom.) It will be easiest if the children are able to tie or buckle their own shoes before they embark on this activity.

Activity

Teach the following song to the class

DIDDLE DIDDLE DUMPLING, MY SON JOHN							
Starting note: F. Count in: 1-2 1-2							
Diddle	diddle	dump	ling,	my	son	John___	
1	2	1	2	1	2	1	2
F	F'	F	F'	F	F'	F	F'
Went	to	bed	with his	trousers		on___.	
1	2	1	2	1	2	1	2
F	F'	F	F'	F	F'	F	F'
One	shoe	off	and	one	shoe	on___.	
1	2	1	2	1	2	1	2
F	F'	F	F'	F	F'	F	F'

Diddle	diddle	dump	ling,	my	son	John___.	
1	2	1	2	1	2	1	2
F	F'	F	F'	F	F'	F	F'

Teach the song to the class. When they can perform it fairly confidently, ask them to walk around the class as they do so, stepping in time to the beat. When they have mastered that, ask each child to take off their right shoe.

Now repeat the exercise making sure that every child starts on the left foot, i.e. the shod foot. To make sure that they are all in step, ask them to stand on their right

81

feet as you count in and then to put their left feet down on the first word. This will need some practice and some children will not master it at this stage. But, with practice, the majority should be able to manage it. Working with fairly small groups can help overcome some of the difficulties. This time, as the children move round, their shod feet will make more sound than the others. Also, because of the lopsided nature of their walk, most children should be able to feel the accent on the shod foot.

Extension

Repeat the activity as above. This time, however, give the children a range of unpitched percussion in two categories, e.g. wooden and metal, wooden and skin. This time, as they walk around they should play their instruments as the shod foot goes down. When they have done this successfully, vary the activity by asking them to play in time with the unshod foot. From here

you can develop the activity further by asking the children with one category of instruments (e.g. wooden instruments) to play on the shod foot and the children with the other type of instruments (e.g. metal instruments) to play on the unshod foot. In this way, some will be playing on the accented beats and the others on the unaccented beats. Make sure that the children continue to sing as they perform these activities, otherwise the synchronisation will be lost.

To extend this further, give one child a low F chime bar and another child a high F (F') chime bar. The one with the low pitched chime bar should play it on the shod foot and the one with the high pitched chime bar should play it on the unshod foot. You could use this activity as a basis for further discussion of the materials from which instruments are made. Examine the ones in the classroom and arrange them into groups such as wooden, metal and skin instruments, etc.

Di - ddle di - ddle dump - ling, my son John

went to bed with his trou - sers on.

One shoe off and one shoe on.

Di - ddle di - ddle dump - ling, my son John.

83. CHIME BARS – LOW TO HIGH ▶

Purpose

To enable children to arrange chime bars in an upward progression on the basis of their sounds and sizes.

Resources

A series of chime bars (start with three: C, D and E); a set of 'steps' made from books arranged at varying heights.

Activity

Arrange the chime bars randomly on the floor in front of the children. Take one of the chime bars and play it. Put it at any point on the steps. Now play the second one. Then play the first and second chime bars in close

succession. Does the sound go up or down? If the sound goes down, put the chime bar on a lower rung on the ladder than the first. If the sound goes up, put the chime bar on a higher rung than the first one. Now play the third chime bar and compare it with the others. Is it higher than both? If so, put it above both of the other chime bars. If it is lower than both, put it on the lowest rung. If the sound is higher than one and lower than the other, then put it in the middle. When the bars have eventually been arranged in the right positions, play a tune going up or going down. This activity could be extended to include many notes.

Another variation of this activity is to give the children the chime bars in random order and ask them to decide which is the longest and which is the shortest. The longer the bar, the lower down on the steps it should be placed. The shorter the bar, the higher it should be positioned. Again, you could start with three

chime bars and build up gradually to several notes. This activity could be extended by asking the children to put the chime bars in order from left to right on the same physical plane.

84. LISTENING TO MARCHES

Listen to a recording of 'When the Saints Go Marching In'. Encourage the children to sing along with it, after they have heard it several times. Then draw their attention to the way that the melody rises and falls in

pitch. The rise in pitch at the outset is particularly evident. You could relate this to the opening of Mendelssohn's 'Wedding March' where there is also a clear rising pitch pattern in the opening fanfare.

85. HICKORY DICKORY DOCK

Purpose
To give the children further practice in moving in time to the beat of a song; to give them further practice in marking the accented beats in a song; to enable them to add simple pitched and unpitched percussion accompaniments to a song; to give them further experience of inventing their own compositions.

Resources
Space for movement; chime bars C and G; chime bars C and high C'; unpitched percussion, e.g. wood blocks, tulip blocks, triangle; cassette: side 2, track 18.

Activity
Teach the children the song.

HICKORY DICKORY DOCK

Starting note: E. Count in: 1-2 1-2

Hickory	dickory	dock,	the
1	2	1	2
C	G	C	G
C	C'	C	C'
Mouse ran	up	the	clock.	The
1	2	1		2
C	G	C		G
C	C'	C		C'

Clock struck	one,	the	mouse ran	down.
1	2	1		2
C	G	C		G
,C	C'	,C		C'
Hickory	dickory	dock		tick
1	2	1		2
C	G	C		G
C	C'	C		C'
Tock	tick	tock		tick
1	2	1		2
C	G	C		G
C	C'	C		C'
Tock.				
C				
C				

When the children have grasped the words and tune of the song, divide the class into groups who mark the beat in a variety of ways. For example,

Group 1: marks the beat with a sound on the wood block as they say 'tick', 'tock' regularly

Group 2: stands and makes a swaying pendulum movement in time to each beat

Group 3: steps round in a circle around the others as they tip-toe mouse-like to the beat of the music
Group 4: marks the beat with a tongue click per beat.

This could be developed further by giving two or four children who are playing the role of mice a chime bar each, tuned (as indicated) to, C and high C'. Those with the lower C could play their note on the first beat each time, while the other children play their note on the second beat. As with the earlier activities of this type, these children should continue to move while performing, otherwise the synchronisation will be affected.

When all these activities are in place, you could add a variation on the accompaniment yourself involving the two notes C and G, as indicated in the middle line of the accompaniment material.

Extension
When the children have mastered the above activities, you could provide a short introduction to the song. At its simplest level, this could be done by asking the instrumentalists to perform for four counts of two (i.e. 1-2 1-2 1-2 1-2) before the singers entered. Do not be afraid to try out other ways of introducing the song. Decide through discussion with the children whether all the instruments should enter together or be added one or two at a time. (Here and elsewhere, it is important to ensure that an accompaniment supports

the singers and does not become so loud that it drowns them out). Therefore do not feel that all the children have to have an instrument at one time. As a general rule, it is better to have more singers than instrumentalists. This does not prevent anyone having a go on the instruments, since you could change the composition of the instrumental groups periodically.

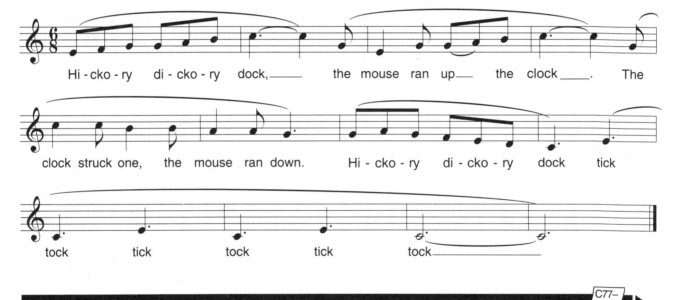

Hi - cko - ry di - cko - ry dock, ____ the mouse ran up __ the clock ____ . The

clock struck one, the mouse ran down. Hi - cko - ry di - cko - ry dock tick

tock tick tock tick tock ____

86. HICKORY DICKORY COMPOSITION

C77–9

Purpose
To give children further experience of creating a simple composition based on a visual stimulus; to give them practice in creating and performing from a score.

Resources
Copymasters 77–9; a range of pitched and unpitched percussion instruments; voices.

Activity
Look at **Copymasters 77–9** outlining the events in the story of 'Hickory dickory dock'.

Discuss the first picture with the children. How will the mouse be moving as it emerges from its hole? (Slowly, carefully, stealthily.) Will it be making a loud or soft sound? (Soft.) What kind of noise will it make? (Squeaking noises, scrabbling or scraping sounds.) What will it hear when it comes into the room? (The clock ticking.) How could this be represented? (With some of the effects already explored in the previous performance activity.) Let the children experiment with various sounds to represent the above. Ask them to perform them to each other. Then decide in what order the sounds should come. Try out various orders and decide on one. Help the children record how that should be played by making drawings of the instruments or by the use of other indicators and reminders such as a coloured shape to indicate a particular effect.

Now examine the second picture. The mouse is going up the clock. How can this be represented? (By means of sounds which rise in pitch, e.g. played on the xylophone.) Will the mouse move quickly or slowly? (Slowly.) Will it be making a loud or a soft sound? (Soft.) Will the clock still be ticking? (Yes.) As with the first picture, encourage the children to experiment with sounds, share them with each other, decide which ones

they are going to use and in what order. Then make a basic score to represent this.

The clock strikes in the next picture. Then the mouse runs down the clock. Again ask the children a series of questions to prompt ideas for sounds, focusing on the type of sounds which might be suitable, their pitch, speed and volume. Then through experimentation and discussion arrive at a score.

Now the various sections can be put together, rehearsed, performed, recorded, played back and, if necessary, altered.

87. PICTURE RHYTHMS WITH SILENCES

C80 –88

Purpose
To give children further experience of applying picture notation to rhymes; to introduce them to ways of notating silence as well as sound in music.

Resources
Copymasters 80–88; cassette: side 2, track 19. You will also need to revise activities 73 and 81.

Activity
So far, you have been involved in helping the children to interpret the notation for musical sounds of different lengths. Music, however, also involves silences which, like sounds, can be of a specific length. Silences in music are called 'rests'. In this activity, you will be helping children to notate such rests. As with other activities in the book, you will start with gestures before moving on to the use of picture rhythm notation.

Seat yourself with the children in a circle. Ask the children to copy you as you tap out a regular beat on your lap. When this has been well established, count in and perform the following rhyme:

1

Count in: 1-2-3-4 1-2-3-4			
I can	see an	el e	phant
1	2	3	4
Si tting	on a	wall	I
1	2	3	4
Do	hope that	el e	phant
1	2	3	4
Does	not	fall.	(Crash!)*
1	2	3	4

* = make a definite one beat gesture in the air so that it does not sound.

(See Copymasters 80–88 for picture notation.)

You can now apply the same principle – of making a silent as well as a sounded one beat gesture – to the following rhymes:

2

Count in: 1-2-3-4 1-2-3-4			
I'm a	li ttle di	ver my	
1	2	3	4
Name	is	Fred.	(Flip*)
1	2	3	4
Ev ery	day I	dive	from the
1	2	3	4
Pi ___	er	Head.	(Flop*)
1	2	3	4

3

Count in: 1-2-3-4 1-2-3-4			
A	corn,	a	corn
1	2	3	4
Fa lling	from the	tree.	(Clonk*)
1	2	3	4
Please	make	sure	that you
1	2	3	4
Don't	land on	me.	(Ouch!*)
1	2	3	4

4

Count in: 1-2-3-4 1-2-3-4			
Crack some eggs,		crack some	eggs.
1	2	3	4
Crack some	eggs for	tea.	(Yum*)
1	2	3	4
Put them	in a	fry - ing	pan and
1	2	3	4
Feed them	all to	me.	(Gulp*)
1	2	3	4

5

Count in: 1-2-3-4 1-2-3-4

Drip	drip	goes the rain.	
1	2	3	4

All	on our	heads.	(Splish*)
1	2	3	4

How I	wish that	I	was
1	2	3	4

Curled up	in my	bed.	(Splosh*)
1	2	3	4

6

Count in: 1-2-3-4 1-2-3-4

Ten	big	sausa	ges
1	2	3	4

Sizzling	in a pan.	(Pop*)	
1	2	3	4

One	goes pop	and the	
1	2	3	4

O ther	goes bang.	(Bang*)	
1	2	3	4

7

Count in: 1-2-3-4 1-2-3-4

Li ttle	Red	Ri ding	Hood
1	2	3	4

Wal king	through the	wood.	(Step)
1	2	3	4

Mind	that	wolf.	He's
1	2	3	4

Up to	no	good.	(Eek!)
1	2	3	4

8

Count in: 1-2-3-4 1-2-3-4

Snow	men,	snow	men
1	2	3	4

Stan ding	in a	row.	(Brrr)
1	2	3	4

When the	sun comes	out	then
1	2	3	4

Where	will you	go?	(Blow!)
1	2	3	4

9

Count in: 1-2-3-4 1-2-3-4

Pu ssy cat,		Pu ssy cat	
1	2	3	4

Where	have you	been?	I've
1	2	3	4

Been	up to	Lon	don to
1	2	3	4

See	the	queen.	(Meow!)
1	2	3	4

Encourage the children to invent appropriate gestures for the silences, for example, rubbing the tummy on 'Yum', patting the head on 'drip', etc. Make sure that, whichever gesture is used, it is a very definite one which lasts for the length of a beat and no longer. As with earlier activities of this type, encourage the children to help you to make up further rhymes and to illustrate them accordingly. Start by using the Copymasters with the words. Then produce versions where the words have been blanked out.

88. BIG CLOCKS AND LITTLE CLOCKS

Purpose
To give children practice in adding a pitched and unpitched percussion accompaniment to a song; to enable them to experience how sounds of different lengths can fit together to create a texture; to introduce them to part singing through performing a round.

Resources
Cassette: side 2, track 20; chime bars, A and D. (Remember that, since there is a short line at the bottom right hand of the letter A, you should choose an A which is lower in pitch than the D.) Unpitched percussion instruments e.g. claves and wood blocks.

Activity
Teach the children the following song:

In this song, the first note starts on the second beat, not the first, as in most of the others which you have taught up until now.

86

BIG CLOCKS AND LITTLE CLOCKS

Starting note: A,.   Count in: 1–2–1–The

1	2	1	2
			The
			A,
Big	clock	goes	tick
1	2	1	2
D	A,	D	A,
tock	tick	tock.	The
1	2	1	2
D	A,	D	A,
Li ttle	clock goes	tick tock tick tock	
1	2	1	2
D	A,	D	A,
tick tock tick tock		tick tock. And so	
1	2	1	2
D	A,	D	A,
All	night	long	I
1	2	1	2
D	A,	D	A,
Can	not	sleep	because
1	2	1	2
D	A,	D	A,
Of	tick	tock	tick
1	2	1	2
D	A,	D	A,
tock_____.			
1	2	1	
D	A,	D	

When the children have mastered the words, add the two note accompaniment on A and D as shown. You might find some children who will be able to play this accompaniment for you.

Extension

You could add an accompaniment using unpitched percussion. Ask the children to repeat the line 'And so all the night I cannot sleep' several times and clap the rhythm.

When they are able to do this accurately, ask them to think the words in their minds and to produce clapping sounds only. When this has also been mastered, arrange for some of the children to play this line on unpitched percussion as an accompaniment throughout the length of the song. A repeated pattern played in this way as an accompaniment is known as an 'ostinato'.

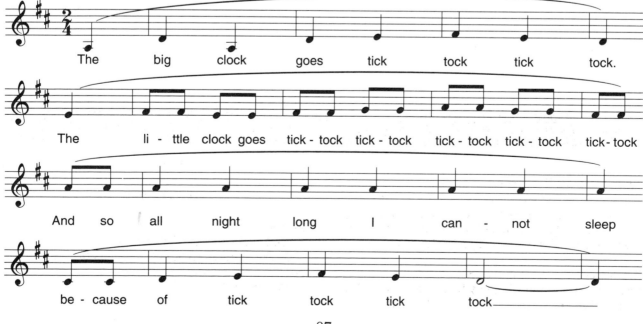

The big clock goes tick tock tick tock.

The li - ttle clock goes tick - tock tick - tock tick - tock tick - tock tick - tock

And so all night long I can - not sleep

be - cause of tick tock tick tock_____

A variety of unpitched instruments could be used for the ostinato. Claves or wood blocks would probably be easiest to handle and would also underline the notion of a ticking clock. If the children want to experiment with other sound sources, however, let them do so and encourage them to discuss the advantages and disadvantages of each. It is important to emphasise, when all the various performers are brought together, that the instruments are there to support and enhance the singing and should not drown out the voices. One or two instrumentalists at a time will be sufficient for this purpose. Remember to ask the instrumentalists to sing along with the others (or at least to sing the words of their ostinato pattern in their heads) otherwise the synchronization will be destroyed.

To extend this activity further, you could arrange for the children to sing it in the form of a round. It could be sung in two, three or four parts, depending on the ability of your pupils. Each new voice should enter after the previous voice has sung the words: 'The big clock goes tick, tock, tick, tock'. You could then add the accompaniments as before.

Do not worry if the children cannot sing the song as a round. You could always return to this activity at a later point. If they can manage this, you could also give them the opportunity to sing well known rounds such as 'Three Blind Mice' or 'Frère Jacques'.

89. MUSIC ABOUT CLOCKS

As a follow up activity, listen to a series of pieces about clocks, e.g. the second movement of Haydn's 'The Clock Symphony' Symphony 101, 'The Musical Clock' from Kodaly's 'Hary Janos Suite'.

Play the pieces to the children several times. Encourage them to move in time with the pulse of the music. Discuss with them the differences in the speed of the clocks. What other differences can they notice in the two musical extracts?

90. COMING NEARER AND MOVING AWAY

Purpose
To heighten children's awareness of the notion of sounds getting louder and softer.

Resources
Space for movement; an unpitched percussion instrument such as a drum or tambour.

Activity
Arrange for one child, or a small group of children, to sit blindfolded in the middle of the room. You, or another member of the class, should now start walking from one end of the room towards the blindfolded child (or children). As you do so, play a repeated beat on the drum at a constant volume. Ask the blindfolded children what they have noticed. They should tell you that the sound of the drum gets louder as you come nearer.

Next, arrange for another child (or group) to sit blindfolded in the middle of the room. Beat a repeated pattern on the drum at a constant volume as before. This time, however, start by standing next to the blindfolded child and moving away. Through questioning, it should be possible to establish that the sound gets softer as you move further away.

A third variation of this game is for the performer to start at one end of the room and move past the blindfolded child to the other end of the room. This will produce an effect of the sound getting louder and then dying away.

Follow up this activity by encouraging the children to listen to the sounds around them and to identify those which get louder, or softer, or louder and then softer, etc. You could make lists of these and add to them as children experience further examples in the world outside the classroom and the school.

91. SOUNDS APPROACHING AND DEPARTING

Listen to pieces describing something coming nearer and moving away again, for example: Elgar, *The Wagon Passes*; Mussorgsky, *Bydlo* from 'Pictures at an Exhibition'.

92. FIRST AND LAST NOTE PITCH GAME

Purpose

To enable children to identify, on the basis of its sound, whether the last note of a short song is higher/lower/same as the first note of the same song.

Resources

Cassette: side 2, track 21; chime bars C, D and E.

Arrange these on a 'ladder' of books as follows:

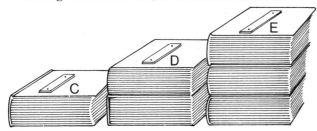

so that the higher the physical position of the note, the higher its pitch.

Activity

Sing the following song to the children:

MERRILY WE ROLL ALONG

Starting note: E.   Count in: 1-2-3-4 1-2-3-4

Me	rri	ly	we	roll	a	long_____,	
1	2	3	4	1	2	3	4
E	D	C	D	E	E	E_____	

Roll	a		long,_____	roll	a	long_____.	
1	2	3	4	1	2	3	4
D	D	D_____	E	E	E_____		

Me	rri	ly	we	roll	a	long_____,	
1	2	3	4	1	2	3	4
E	D	C	D	E	E	E_____	

O	ver	the	deep	blue	sea_____.		
1	2	3	4	1	2	3	4
D	D	D	E	D	C_____		

If you feel sufficiently confident, you could now play it on the chime bars (either with or without the voices). But this is not essential. (Remember though, that the only way to build up confidence is to have a go and also to give yourself plenty of practice before facing a class. Perform to friends and neighbours or in front of the mirror in order to give yourself practice in performing to others.)

Next sing the song again. This time, however, play the chime bar which is the same pitch as the first note (E) and draw the children's attention to precisely which one you played. At the end of the song, ask the children to sing the last note with you. Then invite a child to play each of the chime bars in turn until he or she finds the one which is of the same pitch as the last note. Now discuss with the children whether this last note is higher or lower than the starting note. (It is of course the note C and therefore is lower than the starting note of the song.)

You could play the same game using the following tune and by adding the note F to your ladder of notes:

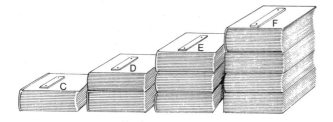

In this case the starting note is C which means that the final note is higher than the starting note. Notice that the song actually starts on the fourth beat.

For an example of a song which starts and finishes on the same note, you could perform 'Twinkle, Twinkle Little Star' or 'Lavender's Blue'. For these two songs, you will need to have a ladder of six notes arranged as follows:

WENT DOWN SOUTH TO SEE MY GAL

Starting note: C. Count in: 1-2-3-4 1-2-3-4

						Oh, I	
1	2	3	4	1	2	3	4
						C	D

Went	down	South	to	see	my	gal,	singing
1	2	3	4	1	2	3	4
E	E	C	D	E	E	C	C	D

Po lly	Wo lly	Doo dle	all	the	way_____.		
1	2	3	4	1	2	3	
E	E	E	E	F	F	E	E	D_____

TWINKLE, TWINKLE LITTLE STAR

Starting note: C

Count in: 1-2-3-4 1-2-3-4

Twin kle,	twin kle	li	tle	star_____.			
1	2	3	4	1	2	3	4
C	C	G	G	A	A	G_____	

How I	won der	what	you	are_____.			
1	2	3	4	1	2	3	4
F	F	E	E	D	D	C_____	

TWINKLE, TWINKLE LITTLE STAR

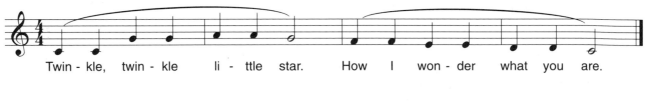

Twin - kle, twin - kle li - ttle star. How I won - der what you are.

LAVENDER'S BLUE

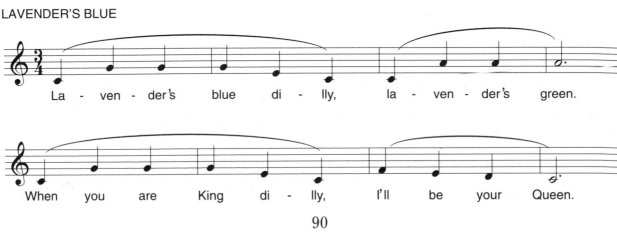

La - ven - der's blue di - lly, la - ven - der's green.

When you are King di - lly, I'll be your Queen.

LAVENDER'S BLUE

Starting note: C.   Count in: 1–2–3 1–2–3

La	ven	der's	blue	di	lly,
1	2	3	1	2	3
C	G	G	E	C	

La	ven	der's	green_____.		
1	2	3	1	2	3
C	A	A	A_____		

When	you	are	king	di	lly,
1	2	3	1	2	3
C	G	G	G	E	C

I'll	be	your	queen_____.		
1	2	3	1	2	3
F	E	D	C_____		

Remember that you do not have to play the tunes on the chime bars in order to be able to play the above games. The important thing is to ensure that the children have the opportunity to be able to test the various chime bars to see whether the first and last notes are the same or different from each other and, if different, to decide how they differ.

Remember also that you do not have to present all the tunes in one go. You could return to various parts of this game at different stages in your course.

93. PICTURE RHYTHMS WITH SILENCES TRANSLATED AS GESTURES

C89 –94

Purpose
To extend children's experience of using picture notations for rhythms; to give them experience of indicating silences using gestures only.

Resources
Copymasters 89–94. This activity follows up the skills learned in activities 66, 73 and 81, so you should revise them again before starting; cassette: side 2, track 22.

Activity
Use **Copymasters 89–94** for picture notation. So far, musical rests have been indicated by silent hand gestures accompanied by an appropriate sound. The same approach is used for the first example below. After that, however, the rests will be indicated by gestures only. Again make sure that the gestures reflect the content of the rhyme and that they are performed strictly in time to the beat. (As in previous sections involving rhythms, do not be afraid to add your own versions and to produce further picture notations for the use of the children.)

You will notice that, here, as earlier, line notation is used as well as pictures. You do not have to use the line notation. You could blank it out. Similarly, at a later stage you might wish to return to these rhymes and rhythmic patterns and make use of the line patterns only or the pictures only.

Count in: 1-2-3-4 1-2-3-4

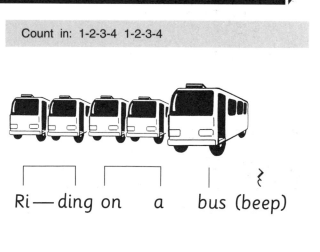

Ri—ding on   a   bus (beep)

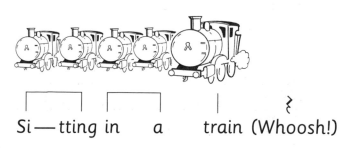

Si—tting in   a   train (Whoosh!)

91

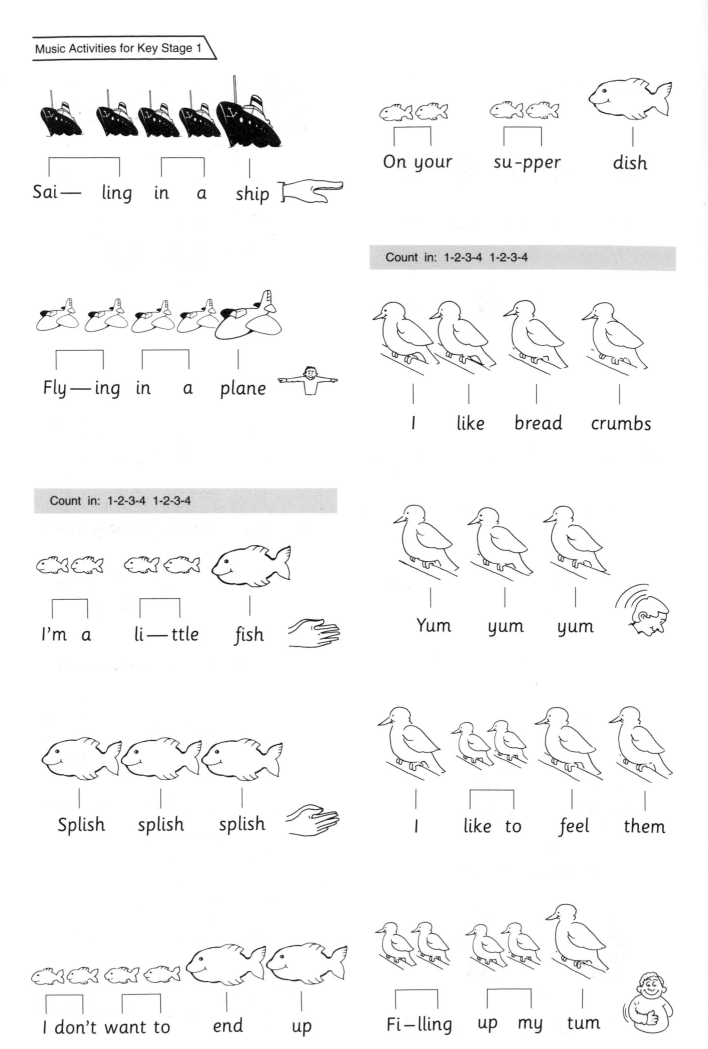

Sai— ling in a ship

On your su-pper dish

Fly—ing in a plane

Count in: 1-2-3-4 1-2-3-4

I like bread crumbs

Count in: 1-2-3-4 1-2-3-4

I'm a li—ttle fish

Yum yum yum

Splish splish splish

I like to feel them

I don't want to end up

Fi—lling up my tum

92

Count in: 1–2 1–2

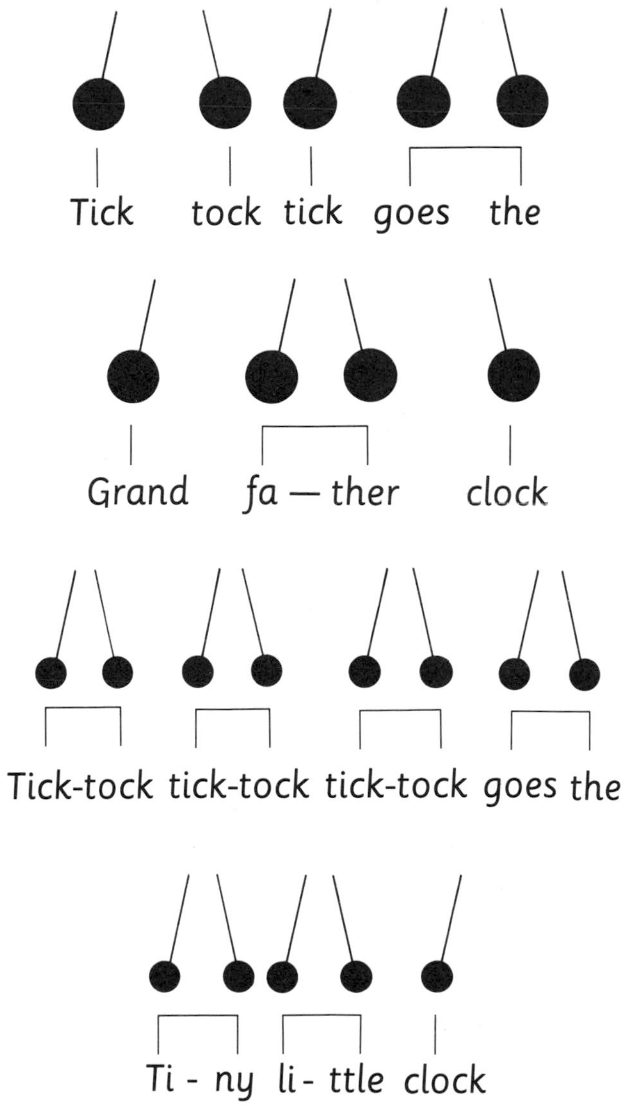

Tick   tock   tick   goes   the

Grand   fa — ther   clock

Tick-tock tick-tock tick-tock goes the

Ti - ny li- ttle clock

Count in: 1–2 1–2

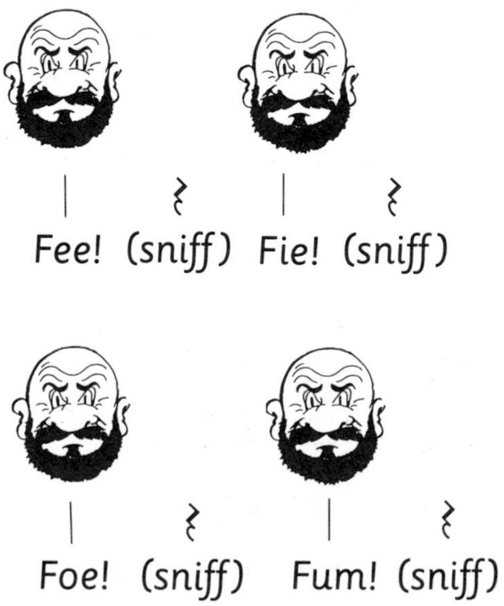

Fee! (sniff) Fie! (sniff)

Foe! (sniff) Fum! (sniff)

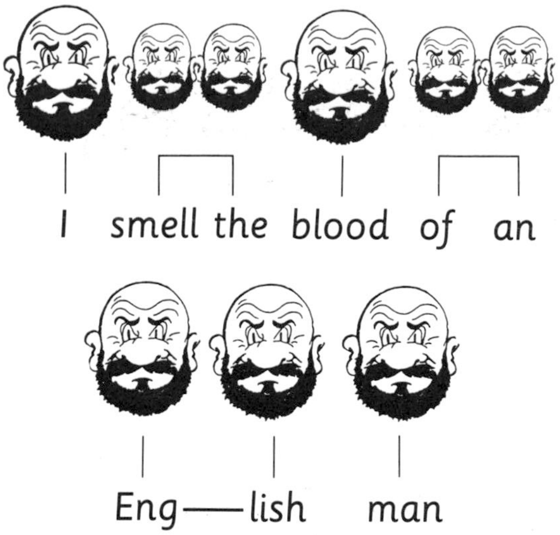

I smell the blood of an

Eng——lish   man

Count in: 1–2–1–2

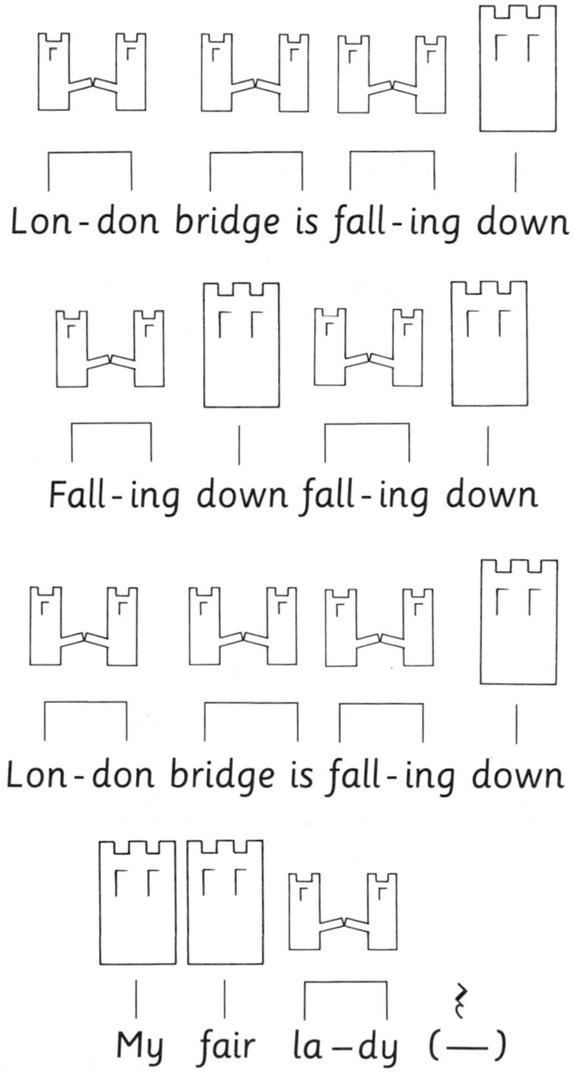

Lon-don bridge is fall-ing down

Fall-ing down fall-ing down

Lon-don bridge is fall-ing down

My fair la—dy (——)

In each of the above, ask the children to clap the rhythms of the words and to make an appropriate gesture on the rests. Suggestions are included in the illustrations.

94. AM I MOVING TOWARDS YOU OR AM I MOVING AWAY?

Purpose
To give children further experience of identifying gradations of volume.

Resources
Space for movement; a tambour or drum.

Activity
Ask a child to sit blindfolded in the middle of the room. Then arrange for a second child to take up position very quietly at a chosen point in the room. The second child now plays the tambour at a constant volume and moves towards or away from the blindfolded classmate who then has to decide, on the basis of the sounds heard, in which direction the performer is travelling.

There are many ways to vary this game. The performer could move towards, then away from and back towards the blindfolded child, etc. The performer could even stay in the same place. Instead of playing an instrument, the performer could sing. With practice, some children might be able to identify the direction of travel of more than one classmate. If this approach is taken, it would be advisable to have the performers playing on instruments with clearly different tone colours.

Extension
Make recordings of various types of vehicles moving towards or away from you. Then ask the children to identify the direction in which the vehicle is moving. At a later stage, they could be asked to identify not only the direction of travel but also the type of vehicle making the sound.

95. PICTURE NOTATION WITHOUT WORDS

C95–104

Purpose
To give children experience of interpreting picture notation unaccompanied by words.

Resources
Copymasters 95–104.

Activity
Make several photocopies of the cats, mice, dogs, cakes and words on Copymasters 95–104 and glue them on to card. To prolong their lifespan, you could also laminate them. Cut the various sections into smaller cards, each with a large single picture on it or a pair of smaller pictures. These could then be arranged in a wide variety of ways to give a range of patterns which the children could clap out.

Count in a steady beat: 1-2-3-4, etc. and ask the children to clap the appropriate pattern. At first you might want to reproduce the rhythmic patterns you have already learnt. But, after a while, you will find that you will have enough confidence to play with the patterns and produce new ones spontaneously while working with the children.

When the children can reproduce the patterns accurately, help them to arrange the cards appropriately to represent one or two sounds per beat. For example, one dog = one sound, two dogs = two sounds per beat.

The above activity involves reading the symbols. If you are going to help your pupils become musically literate, you will also want to give them practice in 'writing' them. The cards which you have made will be a very useful aid.

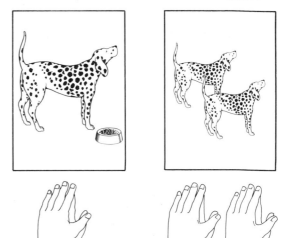

Clap out the patterns which you have learnt earlier to the children or play them the versions on the tape. Ask them to clap them back to you. When they can do this accurately, discuss with them which are the long notes and which are the short ones. Then help them to arrange the pictures into appropriate patterns. When they have done so, ask them to play the rhythm back to you and to decide whether it is exactly the same as the version which they originally heard. As with the previous activity, you will soon gain confidence in making up patterns for yourself. You could extend this activity by using the words 'meow!' 'squeak!' 'woof!' and 'yum' on **Copymasters 99** and **104** to represent rests in the rhythm.

Although all these ideas are presented together here,

do not feel that you have to pursue them all or use every example in one go. Spread the activities out over a period of time. Come back to them. Some children will be able to grasp the ideas quickly. Others will take time. In other words, the rate of progress will be very similar to that found in other areas of the curriculum. As with other areas, work on the principle of little and often – especially when developing this aspect of the music programme. Also remember that the examples presented here are necessarily restricted in number. Do not be afraid to add to them, as you gain more confidence.

96. HUNT THE THIMBLE

Purpose

To develop children's ability to perform and respond to gradations of volume; to give them further practice in being able to identify the pitch relationship between the first and last note of a song.

Resources

Cassette: side 2, track 23.

Activity

Teach the children the following song:

HUNT THE THIMBLE							
Starting note: C. Count in: 1-2-3-4 1-2-3-4							
As	I was	wal	king out	one	day_____		
C	C D	E	G F	E	D_____		
1	2	3	4 1	2	3	4	
I	found a	thim ble	on	my	way_____	.	
B₁	B₁ C	D F	E	D	C_____		
1	2	3 4	1	2	3	4	
I	hid that	thim ble	out of	sight_____	.		
C	C D	E	G F	E	D_____		
1	2	3	4 1	2	3	4	

Can	you		find	it.	You well	might	_____.
B₁	B₁	C	D	F	E	D	C
1	2		3	4	1	2	3	4

When the children are able to perform the song accurately, arrange them in a circle. Put a thimble or another appropriate object behind one of the children. While this is happening, another child should be standing apart from the rest. That child should be blindfolded or at least not be able to see where the thimble is being hidden. When everyone is ready, the children in the circle begin to sing the song. The hunter now enters the circle and as he/she moves towards the thimble the singing should get louder. As the hunter moves further away from the thimble, the singing should get softer. Once the thimble has been discovered, the hunter becomes part of the circle and is replaced by the child who was hiding the thimble. In playing this game, it is important that the children should make the gradations in volume gradual. This will be helped by asking the hunter to move fairly slowly around the circle.

The children will enjoy this game and will want to return to it frequently. On subsequent occasions, try playing the notes indicated under the words. When you can do this fairly fluently, ask the children to identify whether the first and last notes are the same or different from each other. This will reinforce activity 92.

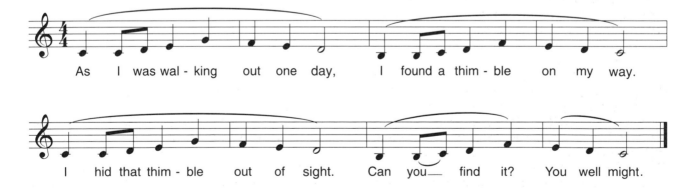

97. SMOOTH SNAKES

Purpose

To introduce children to the notion that melodies can move by step.

Resources

Cassette: side 2, track 24; space for movement; xylophone.

Activity
Teach the children the following song:

THE SNAKE SONG

Starting note: F.   Count in: 1-2 1-2

Snakes__	sli ther	on the	ground__,
1	2	1	2
As they	curl__	round and	round__.
1	2	1	2
In the	sun they	like to	bask__
1	2	1	2
Lying	in the	grass_____.	
1	2	1	2

When they have mastered this song, draw their attention to the way that the tune moves very smoothly from note to note just as a snake moves smoothly. As they sing it, ask them to make smooth movements with their hands down and up as the melody falls and rises.

Extension
Play a series of notes moving upwards and downwards from note to note on the xylophone. As you do so, the children should again match your sounds with appropriate smooth up and downward movements.

When the class has practised this, individual children could take your place at the xylophone.

You could then ask the children to work in pairs. The first child in the pair makes a series of smooth upward and downward arm movements. The second child then has to match these movements with an appropriate movement up and down on the xylophone.

Play the children examples of plainchant. There are several fine recordings of these, particularly by the monks of the Abbey of Solesmes in France. There are also recordings available of plainchant written by the woman composer Hildegard von Bingen.

As the children listen to these performances, draw their attention to the way that for most of the time the music moves very smoothly stepping from note to note. They could match the movement of the sounds with the movements of their hands to emphasize this.

98. LET'S MAKE A CRESCENDO

Purpose
To give children further practice in playing gradations of volume from soft to loud.

Resources
One instrument per child in the class or group.

Activity
Arrange the children in a circle, each with an instrument. One child begins to play at a constant,

moderate volume. Then, one by one, the other children join in until eventually they are all performing. Do this a few times, ensuring that each individual child is keeping to the same volume. Then ask the children to focus on the overall effect. They should notice that the volume actually increases overall, although individually they have been maintaining a constant volume. Point out to them that, as well as having individual players play more loudly, composers also add more instruments together when they wish to produce a louder sound.

99. VOLUME LISTENING ACTIVITY

Begin to make the children aware of the way in which composers build up crescendos by adding instruments together.

Play the children the 'B flat Entr'acte' from Schubert's 'Rosamunde'. Draw their attention to the way that the sound increases in volume when more instruments are playing. Here, and elsewhere, where a piece of music is presented to the children, you could give them a very brief description of who the composer is, where he lived and his country of origin. Do not let this take the place of other activities which focus on the music itself.

When they have listened to the extract a few times, encourage them to move in time to the music, making larger and larger gestures as the volume builds up.

100. LEAPING FROGS

Purpose

To introduce children to the notion that melodies can move by leaps.

Resources

Cassette: side 2, track 25; space for movement; xylophone.

Activity

Teach the children the following song:

THE FROG SONG

Starting note: D. Count in: 1-2 1-2

I'm	a	frog. I	leap	a	round
1		2	1		2
Down and	up and		round and	round.	
1	2		1	2	
When I	leap	in	to	the	air, I'm
1	2		1		2
Here, I'm	there, I'm	ev	ery	where.	
1	2		1		2

When the children have mastered this song, draw their attention to the way that the notes in it leap about, rather than moving smoothly from one note to the next one to it. Ask them to find spaces for themselves around the room. Now, as they sing the song, they should emphasise the leaps in the melody by producing jerky movements up and down to match them.

Extension

Take the xylophone but this time remove alternate bars so that it is impossible to move by step from note to note. Now make up your own jumping tune which the children have to match with appropriate movements. As before, let the children take turns in leading the activity once they have grasped what is required of them.

Again, make sure that the children have experience of converting signs into sounds as well as sounds into signs. To do so, ask individual children to watch a series of movements produced by yourself. These jumpy upward and downward movements should then be converted into a progression of sounds on the xylophone. When they have had sufficient practice at this, let the children work in pairs, with one child producing movements while the second child converts them into matching sounds.

I'm a frog. I leap a-round. Down and up and round and round.

When I leap in-to the air, I'm here, I'm there, I'm eve-ry-where.

101. 'SMOOTH' AND 'LEAPING' MELODIES

Listen to the following sections from Beethoven's Piano Sonatas: the opening of the first movement of 'Sonata in F minor', Op. 2, No. 1; the opening of the First Movement of 'Sonata in C minor', Op. 10, No. 1; the opening of the last movement of the 'Moonlight Sonata'.

In each of those cases you will hear melodies moving by great leaps. You could also draw children's attention to similar features in the following: the opening bars of the first movement of Grieg's 'Piano Concerto'; the opening bars of the first movement of Robert Schumann's 'Piano Concerto'.

You will have noticed that here and elsewhere in the book, you are being urged to draw the children's attention to specific aspects of short sections of pieces. This does not mean, however, that they should be confined to those sections only. Play longer sections of the pieces at times so that the children can get to know them better and begin to build up an awareness of what a wealth of music there is available for them to listen to. As with other activities, you can return to the listening sections again and again and not simply confine them to the point where they appear in the book.

102. LET'S MAKE A DIMINUENDO

Purpose
To give children further experience in playing gradations of volume from loud to soft.

Resources
An instrument for each child in the class or group.

Activity
Arrange the children so that they are sitting in a circle, with an instrument each. When you signal they should all start playing together. Then, at a signal from you, the

players should stop performing one by one, until eventually there is only one child left playing. Practise this a few times, making sure that each child plays at a constant volume. When they can do this competently, draw their attention to the way that the overall sound gradually becomes softer.

If individual children have difficulty in hearing the overall effect, try recording the activity and playing it back to them. But do not rely too heavily on such an approach. It is part of the skill of performing to be able to hear the overall effect of a piece as well as your own contribution to it.

103. STEPS AND LEAPS

Purpose
To enable children to identify combinations of movement by step and by leap within a melody.

Resources
Cassette: side 2, track 26; space for movement; a 'ladder' of chime bars arranged from left to right going upwards in pitch and physical position as follows: C D E F G A B C'. See the illustrations on page 90 on how to create a 'ladder' from piles of books of increasing height.

Arranging the chime bars like this continues to reinforce, visually, the children's association of 'high' and 'low' pitches with a physical position on a ladder of notes. The 'ladder' of course, prepares the children for their later work on reading music notation.

If possible, a set of steps, up and down which the children can move easily and safely.

Activity
Teach the children the following song:

STEP STEP DOWN			
Starting note: E. Count in: 1-2-3-4 1-2-3-4			
Step	step	down_____.	
E	D	C	
1	2	3	4
Step	step	down_____.	
E	D	C	
1	2	3	4
Step	step	down_____.	
G	F	E	
1	2	3	4

Step	step	down_____	and
G	F	E	G
1	2	3	4
Now we	jump both	up and	down. Yes
C' '	B A B	C' C'	G G
1	2	3	4
Round and	round and	up and	down. Oh,
C' C'	B A B	C' C'	G G
1	2	3	4
Watch us	leap both	up and	down then
C' C'	B A B	C' C'	G F
1	2	3	4
Step	step	down_____.	
E	D	C	
1	2	3	4

safely, get some of the children to walk down those at the appropriate points when the music moves by step.

If you have the confidence, you could further reinforce this notion by playing sections of the melody to the children so that they can see how the music moves by step and by leap on the 'musical staircase'.

You could extend this activity further by teaching or reminding the children of 'Twinkle, Twinkle Little Star'. (See page 90.)

TWINKLE, TWINKLE LITTLE STAR

Starting note: C

Count in: 1-2-3-4 1-2-3-4

Twin	kle,	twin	kle	li	tle	star_____.	
C	C	G	G	A	A	G_____	
1	2	3	4	1	2	3	4
How I	won	der	what	you	are_____.		
F	F	E	E	D	D	C_____	
1	2	3	4	1	2	3	4

When they have learnt the song, draw their attention to the way the melody moves. In the first two lines it moves downward by step. In the next two lines, it starts a little higher but again moves downwards by step. In the next three lines, there is a lot of leaping movement before the music returns to the downward steps. You could ask the children to make appropriate movements to illustrate the contour of the melody.

If there are steps available which the children can use

Through discussion and questioning, help the children identify where there is stepwise movement in the melody and where there are leaps. Let them illustrate those with bodily movements. You could also play the melody on the chime bars if you have the confidence. You might find that one or two of the children will also be able to do this.

As a follow up to this activity, encourage the children to reflect on the shape of any melody which they are learning for the first time, or are revising from previous lessons.

104. SPOT THE TUNE FROM ITS SOUND

Purpose

To enable children to identify a tune by listening to its rhythm being tapped out.

Resources

Cassette: side 2; track 27.

Activity

Tap out the following rhythmic patterns to the children and ask them to identify which tune is which. To help you prepare for this activity, the rhythms have been included on the tape.

To make things easier for the children, write out the names of the possible tunes on a series of cards. The children then have to select the ones which they think match the rhythmic pattern heard.

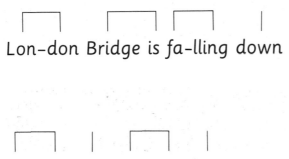

Lon-don Bridge is fa-lling down

Te-ddy bear, te-ddy bear

Frè-re Jacqu-es, Frè-re Jacqu-es

The big clock goes tick tock tick tock

These ideas are merely starters. You can easily add to them, drawing on the repertoire of songs that your particular class has learnt from this book and from other sources.

105. CONDUCTING GAME ▶

Purpose

To give children practice in directing and being directed in group instrumental improvisation; to give them experience of giving shape to such improvisations; to give them the opportunity to reflect on the sounds produced and to select and make suggestions for further approaches to the task set.

Resources

An instrument for each member of the class or group. (Although this activity can be pursued with a whole class, it is probably easier to work with a smaller group at first.)

Activity

Arrange the children so that they are sitting in a semi-circle facing you. Each child has an instrument. Start by asking the children individually to say their names and to clap them out. When they can do this fairly accurately, ask them to play the rhythm on the instruments in front of them. Again check this individually.

Tell them that they are now going to perform as a group. But they are only allowed to start when you indicate that they can do so. At times, you might not want them to play. Therefore they must again stop when you indicate. Show them which hand sign is to be used to bring them in and which is to be used for stopping. Practise the hand signs with the whole group, making sure that they respond to the signs only and that no vocal instructions are given. Point out to them that this is how large groups of performers such as choirs or orchestras operate.

When this has been practised, start your improvisation.

Listen very carefully to the sounds that the children are producing and try to produce variety. Build up the volume by bringing in one child after another. Produce quieter sounds by indicating that some performers should stop. Try creating contrasts of tone colours. For example, you could arrange for a group of wooden instruments to play together for a while, followed by a group of metal instruments. Then both wooden and metal instruments could play together.

Another way to create variety would be to have one or two players performing for a short period, followed by a large group or the group as a whole.

Try also to give an overall shape to the improvisation.

Here are two 'shapes' that you might like to try out:

Shape A
Section 1: One or two performers play on metal instruments.
Section 2: The above performers continue and are joined by three or four wooden instruments.
Section 3: The metal instruments are phased out and more wooden instruments are added.
Section 4: All the instrumentalists play together to form a climax to the piece.

Shape B
Section 1: A small group of skin instruments, such as tambours play together quietly.
Section 2: A group of ringing and shaking instruments join in. After a while, the skin instruments stop playing one by one.
Section 3: The ringing instruments gradually disappear, leaving only the shaking instruments. These are also removed one by one until there is only one sound left.

These are no more than suggestions which you can try out and adapt as you see fit. Having seen the idea, you should have no difficulty in producing a whole range of shapes for yourself.

In the examples given, the children will be tapping out the rhythms of their own names. You could ring the changes by asking them to tap the rhythms of various foods, items of clothing, months of the year, etc.

When pursuing these activities, take time to ensure that the children do respond carefully to your instructions. When a shape has been tried out once, discuss it with the children and help them to see how it can be improved. Then go back to perform it again. Remember to involve the children themselves in discussing the overall effects and in making suggestions

of their own which can then be tried out. A recording of your performance could be a useful tool for such discussion. Alternatively, involve some of the children in the performance and others in careful listening so that they can suggest improvements. You could change the composition of your groups so that everybody has a chance to be both a listener and a performer.

Like other activities in the book, this is an activity to which you can return again and again. As the children gain greater confidence, you will find that they will become more inventive with their suggestions. It is also important to ensure that, once the basic idea and approach have been established, the children themselves are given opportunities to act as the director of the group.

106. FROLICKING FROGS AND SLITHERING SNAKES

C105–7 113, 114

Purpose
To give children practice in performing melodic patterns from picture notation.

Resources
Copymasters 105–7, 113 and 114; Blue tack®; pitched percussion instruments.

Activity
Make several photocopies of the snakes and the frog and mount them on to cards. Arrange these cards in varying combinations at different heights on the board or wall.

Explain to the children that where a snake has its head to the right, it indicates a movement upward by step. Where the snake's head is to the left, the stepwise movement will be downwards. The longer the snake the greater the number of notes involved in the stepwise movement. Also explain to them that the pattern of the

frogs shows melodic leaps upwards and downwards. The wider the gap between the frogs, the greater the melodic leap.

Now you can arrange a large number of different patterns which the children can interpret and play back to you on their pitched instruments. You can use the words 'leap' and 'hiss' on **Copymaster 105** to represent rests, if you wish.

Extension
Make up a melody on a glockenspiel or xylophone and ask the children to listen very carefully to identify where the leaps and the stepwise movements are. On the basis of listening and discussion, they could then arrange the snakes and frogs accordingly.

At a later point, you could give the children written 'scores' of the type found in **Copymasters 113** and **114** to play for themselves. See activity 114.

107. CONDUCTING CRESCENDOS AND DIMINUENDOS

Purpose
To give children practice in directing and being directed in a group instrumental improvisation; to give them experience of giving shape to such improvisations; to give them the opportunity to reflect on the sounds produced and to select and make suggestions for further approaches to the task set; to give them experience of refining such activity by responding to gradations in volume.

Resources
An instrument for each member of the class or group.

Activity
This is an extension of activity 105. This time, however, the conductor should indicate volume changes using a

widening arm movement to indicate an increase in volume and a closing arm movement to indicate a decrease in sound.

Again try to give shape to the improvisations.

You might find the following suggestions helpful:

Shape A
Section 1: All the wooden instruments start playing very quietly.
Section 2: Ringing instruments join them. At a signal from you, the volume increases. At the loudest point indicate that everyone must stop suddenly.
Section 3: After a short pause, everybody starts playing again at a loud volume. Gradually the volume decreases and, one by one, the instruments fall out until there is only one instrument playing.

Section 4: The last remaining instrument gets quieter and quieter until eventually it fades away completely.

Shape B
For this you will need two conductors, each directing half of the instrumentalists.
Section 1: One half of the instrumentalists begin to play quietly. Gradually they build up in volume and then die away again. As they get quieter, the second group begins to play and also to build up gradually.
Section 2: The second group plays loudly and stops. They are then echoed by the first group who play a similar idea quietly. This is repeated.

Section 3: All the instruments play loudly then gradually they become quieter and fade away.
Section 4: There is a short silence. Then suddenly, for one moment, all the instruments play one very loud sound together to mark the end of the piece.

The above are no more than suggested starting points. Experiment with a whole range of shapes but make sure that you involve the children in listening very carefully to themselves and each other and in making suggestions for further approaches.

108. MAKING UP RHYTHMS WITH PICTURE CARDS

C95–104, 108

Purpose
To give children further practice in reading and notating rhythms using rhythm picture cards.

Resources
Copymasters 95–104, 108.

Activity
Make several photocopies of **Copymasters 95–104, 108**, mount them on card and laminate them. Using these cards, you can produce a whole range of different types of rhythm patterns which the children can perform. The children could also take turns in arranging the patterns and leading the activities. As well as sounds, you could involve silences using the pictures

of the crotchet rest provided on **Copymaster 108**.

As in earlier sections, make sure that the children not only convert signs into sounds but also convert sounds into signs. To do so, clap out very short patterns involving the types of rhythms with which the children are familiar. Ask them to clap them back to you, to ensure that they have heard what you clapped accurately. Then, through discussion, help them to arrange the correct pattern of rhythm cards. Finally, clap these back to ensure that the 'written' version is correct.

As well as clapping the patterns indicated, the children should also have the opportunity to transfer them on to instruments.

109. FASTER AND SLOWER

Purpose
To give children practice in performing music which increases and decreases in speed.

Resources
Cassette: side 2; track 28; space for movement.

Activity
Teach the children the following song:

THE LITTLE TRAIN

Starting note: A.   Count in: 1-2-3-4 1-2-3-The

| | | | | | | The |
| | | | | | | 4 |

Li	ttle	train	goes	up	the	hill____,
1	2	3	4	1	2	3	4

| Up | the | hill____, | up | the | hill. | The |
| 1 | 2 | 3 | 4 | 1 | 2 | 3 | 4 |

Li	ttle	train	goes	up	the	hill	and
1	2	3	4	1	2	3	4

| Just | gets | to | the | top_____. |
| 1 | 2 | 3 | 4 | 1 | 2 |

2nd verse
And now it's going down again
Down again, down again. And
Now it's going down again. Oh,
Will it ever stop?

3rd verse
Now watch it running on the rails
On the rails on the rails. Now
Watch it running on the rails. Past
Houses, church and shop.

4th verse
At last it's slowing down again
Down again down again. At
Last it's slowing down again. And it's
Come to a stop.

When the children have learnt the song, let them make a train by standing in a line behind each other, each child holding on to the waist of the child in front.

As they sing the song they move round the room. On the first verse, they should gradually get slower and slower. On the second verse they should speed up. The third verse is performed at a constant, fairly quick speed. Then, on the last verse, as the train comes into the station, it should slow down and eventually come to a stop.

The li - ttle train goes up the hill, up the hill, up the hill. The li - ttle train goes up the hill and just gets to the top.

110. TRAINS IN MUSIC

Listen to the representation of trains in: 'Pacific 231' by Honegger, and 'The Little Train of the Caipira' by Villa-Lobos. Draw the children's attention particularly to the gradations in speed within these pieces.

111. FORTE, PIANO, CRESCENDO AND DIMINUENDO

C109 -112

Purpose
To introduce children to the conventional signs for loud, soft, getting louder and getting softer; to give them practice in applying these signs in an improvisation.

Resources
Copymasters 109–112.

Activity
Make several photocopies of **Copymasters 109–112**, mount them onto card and laminate them.

Introduce each card to the children in turn pointing out that:

f = loud
p = soft
$<$ = getting gradually louder
$>$ = getting gradually softer

Revise activity 107. This time, instead of using hand signs, the conductor(s) could hold up a card as appropriate.

Introduce each card gradually into the activities to ensure that the children do not become confused. Eventually you will be able to use all the cards in an improvisation and you will be able to entrust the leadership and their selection to the children themselves.

112. RHYTHMIC PATTERNS IN MORE THAN ONE PART

C115 –117

Purpose
To give children practice in performing more than one part using picture rhythms.

Resources
Copymasters 115–117.

Activity
The approach will be the same as for activity 108. This time, however, present two sets of rhythmic patterns set one above the other. One child, or group, should perform the upper line while a second child, or group, performs the lower line. To ensure accuracy, it is best to practise each part separately before combing them. Use differing pictures to help children identify their parts.

As with the previous activities of this type, you will need to return to it on many occasions to enable the children to develop fluency in it.

113. TWO PART INVENTIONS

Listen to any one of J S Bach's 'Two Part Inventions' for keyboard. Point out to the children that, just like the pieces they have been performing, these inventions also have two 'lines' of music.

Each line 'imitates' the other by having a similar tone and rhythm. This is rather like having two twins running after each other: one starts and then the other follows.

114. TUNEFUL PICTURES

C113 –114

Purpose
To give children further practice in identifying the contours of melodies.

Resources
Copymasters 113–114; chime bars arranged on a ladder of books as in activity 105.

Activity
Remind the children of the way that, in earlier activities, they were involved in indicating the shapes of melodies using leaping frogs (for leaps) and slithering snakes (for smooth stepwise movements).

Now draw their attention to the first line drawing on **Copymaster 113**. They will notice that, at each angle of the house there is a dot. These dots represent notes. There are three different notes in all. The first and the last notes (at the base of the building) are the same. The two notes at the base of the roof are also the same. The remaining note is the one at the pinnacle of the roof. These three notes will be at different heights. The first note is the lowest. The one for the base of the roof is

slightly higher and the one at the top of the roof is the highest. Choose three notes to represent these. You could, for example use C E A. In that case, you would 'play' the house as follows: C E A E C.

In the same way – using the notes C E A high C' – you could play the church as follows: C A C A E E C.

Of course, these are not the only notes you could use. The important point to remember is that the notes should be at appropriate pitches to reflect the different heights of the notes in the drawings.

Once they have understood the principle, the children will then be able to convert the pyramids, the boat and the tree into melodies. You could also work with them on producing their own musical drawings.

As an extension of this activity, you could present the children with several pictures and play a sequence which corresponds to one of the drawings. The children would then have to identify which picture was being played.

This activity offers numerous possibilities, to which you can keep returning.

115. PLAYING AS A BAND

Purpose

To give children further experience of playing instruments using picture indicators; to enable them to combine the patterns to produce an ensemble performance.

Resources

Copymaster 115.

Activity

Make several photocopies of **Copymaster 115**. Laminate them and cut them into three vertical strips. The first strip will have the triangle part on it. The second will have the tambourine part and the third the drum part.

Give the children the tambourine part. Look at this carefully and discuss it with them. They will notice that the first square has two small tambourines. Therefore these will be short sounds. The remaining three are large tambourines. These will each be a beat long. Now practise it with the children – firstly by clapping it and then by playing it on a tambourine. They could take turns with this as the others clap. Remember to count in four beats before you start and make sure that the children play strictly in time with the beat when they are performing.

When they have mastered this, do the same to the triangle line and to the drum line. These are also included on the tape to help you.

When each part has been learnt, arrange for all the players to perform the three parts together. It is particularly important to count in: 1–2–3–4 and to maintain a steady clapping beat yourself while they do this.

116. COMPOSING USING FAST AND SLOW SOUNDS

Purpose

To give children further experience of composing, using different speeds as a stimulus.

Resources

Space for movement (this activity is probably best pursued in the school hall or at least in a large space); a range of pitched and unpitched percussion instruments. Arrange these so that there are several groups of four or five instruments set fairly wide apart in the room. The composition of each instrumental group is for you to decide. You might, for example, decide to have matching groups of instruments or some groups of metal instruments and some group of wooden ones, etc.

Activity

Arrange the children around the room. Beat a regular pulse on a tambour and ask the children to travel round the room in various directions in time to the beat. Remind them not to bump into each other. When they have mastered this, vary the speed of the tambour beat. They must then respond by moving more quickly or more slowly accordingly.

When they are able to do this in a controlled way, ask them to take their places at the groups of instruments. Give each group a number. Ask the even numbered groups to produce a short piece of music which consists of very slow sounds. Ask the odd numbered groups to produce a short piece consisting of very fast sounds.

To ensure that the whole activity does not end in chaos, make sure that you have a clear procedure for starting and stopping the activity. A cymbal clash, for example could indicate that everyone must stop immediately and put their instruments – including any beaters – on the floor immediately. Unless you insist on this, particularly the putting down of beaters, you will drive yourself insane. Practise this procedure of starting and stopping several times and insist on its being strictly applied.

The children should work on their pieces, trying out ideas for about five minutes. Then tell them that now they have tried out various ideas, they must choose exactly which sounds that they are going to use because they will shortly be required to play them to each other.

Give them another two or three minutes to practise what they are going to perform. At the end of that period, stop them and explain that each group will now be asked to play. When a group is playing, all the rest must listen very carefully and decide on something which they particularly like about the piece which they are hearing. Make sure that you also listen along with the children to set them an example of how to listen with concentration. To help the listeners, and also to ensure that what is being performed is intentional and not just a series of accidents, ask each group to play twice. Insist on silence before they start and also for a moment at the end of the performance so that it is given a clear setting. You frame music with silence just as you frame a picture. In that way you make them both special.

When a piece has been performed, ask the children to tell you what they liked about it. Later, when they have gained more confidence with the activity, you could also ask how they think the piece might be improved. To ensure that the criticism is constructive, start by asking the performers themselves to criticise their own work. The types of improvements which might be made tend to be fairly predictable, e.g.

105

● ensuring that the piece has a clear ending and that the children know when to finish

● making sure that everyone is not playing all the time. Remind them of how, in earlier improvisations, individuals came in or were phased out at different times.

● making use of occasional silences. Children and adults, when they start on this type of activity, often forget that music involves silence as well as sound and that a well placed silence can make a definite effect.

● ensuring that the slow sections really are played slowly. Children often have difficulty in playing slowly. One way to overcome this, if you are using chime bars, is to space the chime bars at a distance from each other so that the children have to travel from one to the other.

Other ideas will occur to you or will be suggested by the children. Do not be in too much of a rush to offer your own suggestions. Encourage the children to discuss ideas since they are the composers. You should be the catalyst.

After hearing two or three of the pieces, ask the children to go back to their pieces and redraft them using some of the ideas suggested. By that stage, others who have not yet performed will have thought of ways to improve their pieces along similar lines. Therefore, at that point, do not worry if you have not heard everyone. The groups which have not yet been heard can go first next time and they will have had the benefit of hearing other suggestions being made which they can use to improve their own pieces.

Just as in P.E., a lesson of this type needs to be presented at a good pace.

Extension

At a later point, when the ideas have been refined, odd numbered groups could be paired with even numbered groups. Using the existing ideas, these groups could then experiment with producing patterns based on fast and slow music.

117. PLAYING AS A BAND 2

C116 –117

Purpose
To give children further experience of playing instruments using picture indicators; to enable them to combine the patterns to produce an ensemble performance.

Resources
Copymasters 116–117.

Activity
In presenting this section, you could adopt the same approach as that already outlined in activity 115.

This type of activity takes time to master. Therefore do not be too disappointed if the children do not succeed in playing together immediately. Be patient to take time to ensure that each individual part is being played correctly and in time with the beat. Then combine this with another line and another until the whole performance is in place.

118. COMPOSING USING LOUD AND SOFT SOUNDS

Purpose
To give children experience of composing, using differences of volume as a stimulus; to introduce ways to indicate the shape or form of their compositions.

Resources
You will need a range of pitched and unpitched percussion instruments. Arrange these so that there are several groups of four or five instruments set fairly wide apart in the room. The composition of each instrumental group is for you to decide. You might, for example, decide to have matching groups of instruments or some groups of metal instruments and some group of wooden ones, etc. You will also need a series of mathematical shapes, either 2D or 3D.

Activity
The basic approach here will be the same as that described in detail in activity 116. This time, ask the odd numbered groups to produce pieces based on soft sounds and the even numbered groups to focus on loud

sounds. From here, the children can progress to the stage where they are experimenting with shapes and patterns based on various combinations of loud and soft sounds.

At this point, the children could notate these patterns very simply by choosing a mathematical shape to represent various sections of their music. Thus a triangle might represent a loud section and a circle a soft one. Give the children several examples of each shape. By manipulating these they can produce various types of 'score', play them and discuss the relative effectiveness of each.

119. IDENTIFYING LIKE AND UNLIKE PHRASES IN MELODIES

Purpose
To enable children to identify like and unlike phrases in melodies.

Resources
A series of mathematical shapes such as those on Copymasters 119 and 120.

Activity
Sing 'Three Blind Mice' with the children. When they have done this a few times, draw their attention to the shape of the tune. The first two lines have the same tune. Choose two identical shapes (e.g. two circles) to represent this. The next two lines are also similar but they are slightly higher in pitch. You could again use two circles. But, to highlight the slight difference, the children could colour these two circles. The next three lines are the same as each other but different from the opening. These could be represented by three squares, for example. Finally, the last line is the same as the first and can therefore be represented once more by an uncoloured circle.

After guiding the children through this, you could ask them to sing other tunes which they know well and ask them to analyse the shape of those in the same way.

'Jack and Jill', for example has the following shape.

Lines 1 and 2 = one shape;
lines 3 and 4 = a contrasting shape.

'Hickory Dickory Dock' has the following pattern

Line 1 = one shape (e.g. square)
Line 2 = same shape (= square)
Line 3 = new shape (e.g. triangle)
Line 4 = further new shape (e.g. circle).

120. INSTRUMENTAL AND VOCAL PERFORMANCE

C118 –120

Purpose
To enable children to read and perform rhythmic picture notation; to use these patterns as an instrumental accompaniment to a song; to give children further practice in analysing the shape of a melody; to give them the opportunity to compose a new piece to the same shape as that of a song which they have analysed.

Resources
Copymasters 118–120; cassette: side 2, track 7; drum, claves, and cymbals.

Activity
Revise the song 'London Bridge is Falling Down' with the children. Then take the drum line and clap this out on the strong beats as indicated. When this has been mastered, one or two of the children can transfer it to the actual instrument. Now repeat the approach for the claves and finally the cymbal part.

When all the instrumental parts have been learnt, make sure that there is an appropriate balance in the music and that the vocal line is being accompanied, not overpowered, by the instruments.

You could extend this activity further by asking the children to identify the pattern of the tune.

It could be represented as follows using the copymasters.

Line 1 = circle
Line 2 = square
Line 3 = circle
Line 4 = triangle (or possibly a coloured square since it is fairly reminiscent of the second line.)

Having analysed this shape, the children could then be asked to produce a composition with the same shape. The circles could, for example, be slow sections. The square could be a fast section and the triangle could be a section which starts quickly and then slows down towards the end. Alternatively, the various shapes could be used to represent differences of volume.

GLOSSARY OF MUSICAL TERMS

Accent
Imitate the sound of a clock ticking. Say 'tick, tock, tick, tock' regularly. Now repeat the exercise and clap every time you say 'tick'. The 'tick' now sounds louder than the sounds next to it. Therefore it is said to be an accented sound. In music, an accented note is one which is louder and given greater emphasis than others.

Accompaniment
The accompaniment is the 'backing' to a performer or group of performers. If you sing a folk song and someone plays the guitar along with you, the guitar is said to be providing the accompaniment. It is possible to be accompanied by others or to accompany yourself. It is also possible for the accompaniment to be provided by a large number of instruments. In an opera, for example, the accompaniment is often provided by a full orchestra.

Arranging
Arranging is the process of taking an existing piece of music and developing it in some way. For example, a well known pop song might have its words removed and be arranged so that it is played by instruments only. Another example might be to add an accompaniment to a solo tune.

Beat (or pulse)
When you listen to a piece of music, you often find yourself tapping your feet or moving your head regularly with it, rather as if you were a clock. When you do this, you are reacting to the underlying beat or pulse of the music. When soldiers march to music, they move in time to the beat. Not all music has a regular beat or pulse. If you listen to church music from the Medieval period, for example, you will not find it very easy to feel a steady beat.

Composing
This is the act of thinking up musical ideas, putting them together and building them up into an original piece of music.

Dynamics
This is the term used to refer to the loudness or softness of sounds. Therefore, when a conductor tells a group of performers to 'notice the dynamics', he or she is asking them to make sure that they are paying attention to the differences in volume indicated by the composer.

Dynamics are traditionally indicated by a series of signs, e.g.

ff: very loud
f: loud
mf: moderately loud
mp: moderately soft
p: soft
pp: very soft.

Elements
These are the building blocks of music such as pitch, duration, pace, timbre, texture, dynamics, and structure.

Glissando
If you take a beater and slide it from left to right or right to left on a xylophone or glockenspiel, it produces a rapid sequence of notes. This known as a 'glissando'. You can produce a glissando on the piano by sliding the back of your fingers rapidly up or down the keys.

Harmony
Harmony is produced when two or more sounds are performed at the same time.

High or low notes
You will find high notes on the right hand side of the piano; low ones on the left. In staff notation, the higher the pitch of a note, the higher it is placed on the stave. The lower its pitch, the lower its position will be. In this way, the stave acts as a kind of graph to show the rise and fall of the musical pitches.

Improvise
This is the word applied to the process of making up the music as you are performing. Jazz musicians make a great use of improvisation.

Melody
A melody is a series of sounds which move upwards or downwards or are repeated to produce a tune.

Ostinato
If you play a series of notes over and over again as an accompaniment to a melody, this is known as playing an 'ostinato'.

Pace
This refers to the speed at which the underlying beat of a piece of music goes and is also referred to by the Italian word, *tempo.*

Phrase
Listen to a singer performing. The singer does not keep singing a series of notes which go on indefinitely. Every now and again, he or she will take a quick breath or sing a slightly longer note or come to a short stop. This breaks up the music in much the same way that we break up speech so that we do not sound like Daleks. These sections into which music is divided are known as

phrases. It is not only singers who produce phrases in music. You will also notice the same effect if you listen to instrumentalists performing.

Pitch
We use the term pitch when we are referring to whether notes are high or low notes.

Pitched (or tuned) percussion
These are percussion instruments which have notes of different pitches and on which it is therefore possible to play tunes. Please see the introductory section to the book, where you will find details of the types of pitched percussion instruments commonly available.

Pulse
See *Beat*.

Repetition
When two or more notes in a row are at the same pitch, they are said to be repeated. A collection of notes, or a particular rhythmic pattern, can be repeated as can a whole section of music.

Rhythm
This refers to the way that long notes, short notes and silences are combined in music.

Rhythmic pattern
A group of long and short sounds.

Scale
A scale is a basic group of notes from which a melody or longer piece of music can be built. There are probably as many different types of scales as there are languages and dialects in the world. Many of the tunes in this book are built on what is known as a major scale. To play an example of a major scale arrange your chime bars as follows:

    C D E F G A B C

(Each bar should be slightly smaller than the one to its left. The letter names of the notes are stamped on the bars themselves.) If you now play each note in sequence from left to right you will be playing what is known as a C major scale. If you want to play the same scale on the piano, this is what you do:

i. Look at the black notes. You will notice these are arranged in alternating groups of two and three notes.
ii. Choose one group of two black notes.
iii. Look for the white note immediately to the left of the lower of the two black notes.
iv. Starting with that note and moving from left to right play the eight white notes next to each other in order.

Signs
The length or pitch of a note can be shown through a number of visual indications. A high note, for example, could be indicated by holding the arms high in the air and a low note by crouching down. In the same way, a group of three short notes and a long note could be shown by arranging a series of objects, such as building blocks as follows: ☐ ☐ ☐ ▭

Structure
This refers to the way that a piece of music has been put together so that some sections are the same as, or contrast with, others.

Style
Dress designers use particular patterns to produce garments which are individual to them. From one historical period to another and from one country to another, styles of dress change. The same is true of music. The way in which a composer puts together the elements of music results in a particular style. This can vary from one composer to another, from one generation to another and from one country to another.

Symbols
These are the written signs used to show which notes are to be performed, at what pitch, for how long, how loudly or quietly, on their own or with other notes, how quickly or slowly. There are many different types of symbols used in music, e.g. staff notation, graphic notation, solfa, chord indications, etc. In this book, the symbols used often take the form of pictures of large and small objects. This is a useful way of introducing young children to the relevant musical concepts.

Texture
Texture refers to the way that sounds and melodies are combined and blended together in music. Sometimes, the texture will be such that a particular melody is heard as being more important than any of the other sounds being performed. At other times, there might be several instruments playing together, every one of which seems to have an equally important tune to play. This is very similar to the situation in textiles where sometimes one colour or a particular type of fabric is made to stand out from the others. At other times, all the elements are equally important and the material is smooth and closely woven.

Timbre/tone colour
Imagine a note of the same pitch and length being sung by a man, a woman, or a child, and being played on the violin, the trumpet and the piano. The note would not change in pitch or length but its quality would change so that you would hardly be likely to think that the male voice was the sound of a trumpet. This distinctive quality of a sound is known as its 'timbre'. The term 'tone colour' is also sometimes used to describe it.

Unison
Sing 'Three Blind Mice'. Now sing it along with someone else. When two or more people perform the same tune at the same time and in the same way, they are said to be performing in unison. This is different from 'harmony' where two or more people perform together but perform different notes from each other.

Unpitched (or untuned) percussion
These are percussion instruments on which it is not possible to play tunes.

Copymaster 12

I can see an el — e- phant

Si — tting on a wall I

Do hope that el — e- phant

Does not fall. (Crash!)

Copymaster 80

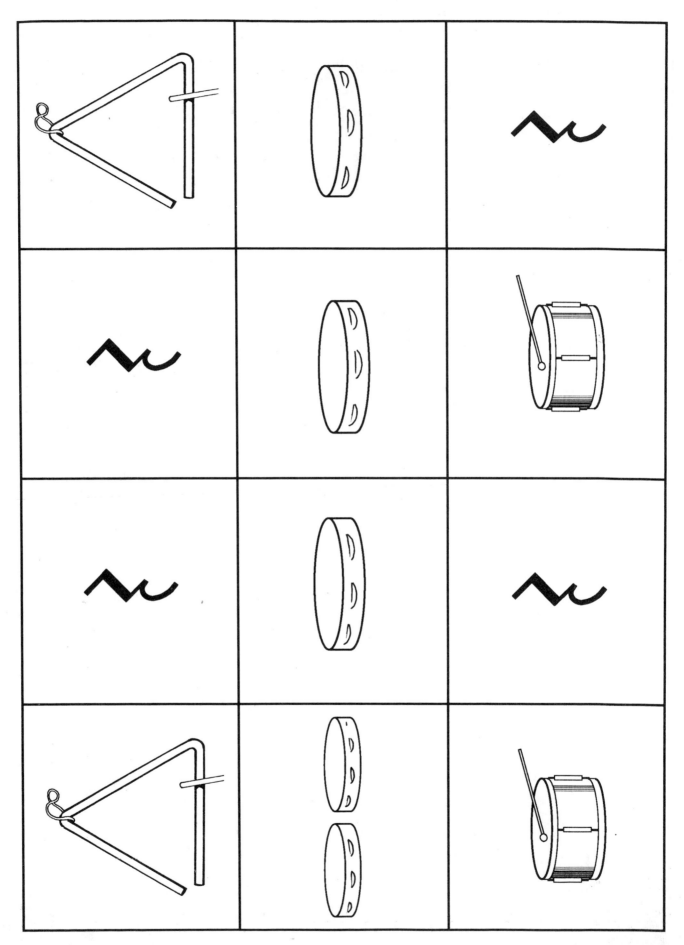